THE REFERENCE SHELF (*Continued*)

SO-BJL-124

Volume XX

No.
5. Federal World Government. J. E. Johnsen. $1.50.
6. Federal Information Controls in Peacetime. R. E. Summers. $1.50.

No.
7. Should the Communist Party Be Outlawed? J. E. Johnsen. $1.50.

Volume XIX

No.
3. Free Medical Care. C. A. Peters. $1.25.

No.
5. United Nations or World Government. J. E. Johnsen. 75c.

Volume XVIII

No.
3. Representative American Speeches: 1945-1946. A. C. Baird. $1.25.
5. Anatomy of Racial Intolerance. G. B. de Huszar. $1.25.

No.
6. Palestine: Jewish Homeland? J. E. Johnsen. $1.25.

Volume XVII

No.
4. Representative American Speeches: 1943-1944. A. C. Baird. $1.25.

No.
5. Lowering the Voting Age. J. E. Johnsen. $1.25.

Volume XVI

No.
1. Representative American Speeches: 1941-1942. A. C. Baird. $1.25.
2. Plans for a Postwar World. J. E. Johnsen. 50c.

No.
6. Representative American Speeches: 1942-1943. A. C. Baird. $1.25.
7. Reconstituting the League of Nations. J. E. Johnsen. 50c.

Volume XV

No.
1. Representative American Speeches: 1940-1941. A. C. Baird. $1.25.
3. Federal Regulation of Labor Unions. J. V. Garland. $1.25.
7. The Closed Shop. J. E. Johnsen. $1.25.

No.
9. Permanent Price Control Policy. J. E. Johnsen. $1.25.
10. A Federal Sales Tax. E. R. Nichols. $1.25.

WITHDRAWN

CONCORDIA UNIVERSITY

HE8698.M3   C001 V
TELEVISION AND RADIO IN AMERICAN LI

3 4211 000039562

THE REFERENCE SHELF

Vol. 25   No. 2

TELEVISION AND RADIO
IN AMERICAN LIFE

Edited by
HERBERT L. MARX, JR.

THE H. W. WILSON COMPANY
NEW YORK   1953

KLINCK MEMORIAL LIBRARY
Concordia Teachers College
River Forest. Illinois

Copyright 1953
By The H. W. Wilson Company
Printed in the United States of America
Library of Congress Catalog Card No. 53-5514

39058

PREFACE

As the television set assumes its place beside—or in place of —the radio receiver in growing millions of American homes, it seems appropriate to examine the place of broadcasting in American life today. Americans have a knack of accepting new mechanical or electronic wonders almost as natural developments. So swift is the pace of acceptance of new items that the electric refrigerator is now old-fashioned if it does not defrost itself, and the clothes washer is virtually useless if it cannot operate itself and turn itself off. Hardly has television reached most major United States population centers when it becomes almost a necessity for the "pioneer" television families to have a second set for the children's bedroom or recreation room.

Thus, television has moved in with little opportunity for us to assess its place in American life. Of course, there have been many surveys, studies, and scare statistics—the vast majority of them based on only the earliest reaction to the new communications medium in a small area. By now, however, television is no longer a novelty in many places, and we can make some solid judgments.

This volume, as indicated by the opening section, places first emphasis on television, rather than radio, but throughout an attempt is made to judge the total effect of broadcasting—through both microphone and camera—on American life. As to technical matters, this material touches only lightly on a few of the newer aspects of TV, such as subscription television. Nor is the book concerned with broadcasting as a psychological weapon in the "cold war." For this, see *America's Weapons of Psychological Warfare* (edited by Robert E. Summers, The Reference Shelf, v23, no4). The volume is confined to a study of broadcasting to the home and school, with the exception of a brief discussion, in its relation to advertising, of broadcasting to public transportation vehicles (see articles on "The 'Captive' Audience").

With television spreading so quickly, most statistics are of only fleeting use. Here, however, are some pertinent figures. At the end of 1952, according to a Radio Corporation of America study, there were 21 million American homes equipped with television—a rise of six million in one year.[1] This means that just under one out of two families in the nation has a television set. In December 1952, there were 117 television stations on the air, with construction permits granted for another 135.

Estimates on the number of radio sets in use range from 103 to 105 million, with at least one in virtually every home. According to the Federal Communications Commission, there were 2331 standard (AM) radio stations and 637 frequency modulation (FM) radio stations in operation in 1952.

One final statistical thought: With 6.3 per cent of the world's population, the United States has more than half of the world's radio sets, and a far larger share of its television sets. With such wealth, what kind of job is our democratic system of broadcasting doing? That is the main theme of this volume.

The editor expresses herewith special thanks for copious material to the Federal Communications Commission, the National Association of Radio and Television Broadcasters, and the Joint Committee on Educational Television. Acknowledgment is also gratefully made to the many authors and publishers who granted permission to reprint materials.

HERBERT L. MARX, JR.

February 16, 1953

[1] From year-end statement by David Sarnoff, Chairman of the Board, Radio Corporation of America. RCA. New York. Released December 29, 1952.

CONTENTS

TELEVISION TAKES OVER

EDITOR'S INTRODUCTION

The widespread, rapid growth of television has made the new medium the subject of countless surveys—most of them taken in a limited area where the impact of TV is so new that the resulting statistics are startling but useless. But the fact that there have been so many surveys tells us for certain that television has "taken over," at least for the present.

The articles in this section avoid the view taken at too close range. They are intended to tell something of the longer term effects of television on American life.

The effect of TV on the motion picture industry, the theatre, and on spectator sports is important. But it would seem that the American genius for adding one more item to our high standard of living without having to dispense with any other item applies to television today—as it did to radio a generation ago. In other words, we are becoming a nation of television viewers, without eliminating other leisure-time activities to any great extent.

Radio broadcasting has been hard hit by television. But the radio networks, and in some cases radio stations themselves, control most TV stations. Thus the changing emphasis from radio to television has been comparable to a manufacturer concentrating on a new product in place of an older one.

Television has thrust farther into the background one of the most promising experiments of post-World War II days—the rise of small, independently owned frequency modulation (FM) radio stations. Designed to reach a limited area with high fidelity quality, FM seemed the complete answer for those whose listening interests differ from the majority. But many brave, new FM stations have found it impossible to make the grade financially. There were 53 authorized FM stations in 1945. This rose to 1020 in 1948, and has since dropped to fewer than 700.

Television is not alone responsible for the disappointing progress of frequency modulation broadcasting. But it certainly has diverted energy and money which might otherwise have been channeled to FM.

TV'S EFFECT ON FAMILY LIFE [1]

After five years [1948-52] of checking the effect of television on family life in our test city, "Videotown," we have yet to find any evidence to substantiate the theory that interest in television will subside in the average home. Neither set usage (hours set is tuned in) nor persons viewing has fallen. Set usage remains at the same high level as . . . [1951]—86 per cent in use during weekday evening hours. Average hours viewing per person are greater; older sets are used over a half hour longer each evening than are new sets; owners of older sets sit in front of their sets longer than new owners.

There is a slight decline since . . . [1951] among families with older sets, in the number of people who watch television on any average weekday night, but those who do watch are watching almost a half hour longer than they did a year ago. The combination of an equal number of sets tuned in, for more hours, but fewer watching is the result of a revolving family audience with greater individual program selectivity.

The only indications that a peak of viewing may have been reached during evening hours are found in the fact that set usage and hours of viewing per person are less for newer than older sets. With older sets tuned in an average of five out of seven available evening hours, it would seem almost impossible for them to show further increases. In other words, averages may tend to level off or fall as the market becomes more saturated due to habits of new set owners. The other indication of a peak is a slight falling off of viewing among children. The adults in the family, rather than the children, are . . . holding up the average.

[1] From *Videotown—V; Fifth Annual Census on Television and Its Effect on Family Life*. Cunningham and Walsh, Inc. New York. 1952. p 1-6. Reprinted by permission.

Videotown . . . is actually New Brunswick, New Jersey. This city was chosen as the . . . test laboratory for TV because it is a normal marketing and manufacturing area, not primarily a suburb of New York, yet near enough for good reception from the many New York TV stations. The history of Videotown is the story of what has happened in other multistation TV markets, and the story of what will happen in the rest of the country as greater program selection becomes available through the addition of new stations.

Television, young when measured in years, has already reached maturity in Videotown and other multistation cities. This rapid development from infancy to maturity has not been equaled by any other major industry in its formative years.

This rapid growth of TV has two aspects. One . . . is increase in set saturation, its first very rapid growth, its declining rate. The other is the impact of TV on activities, habits, and lives of viewers.

Long hours of viewing have necessarily had an important effect on the lives of set-owning families during weekday evenings. (This study, remember, does *not* cover Saturday or Sunday nor, in detail, daytime activity.) Probably the most drastic effect has been on movies and radio, the two industries with which TV competes most directly.

In 1950 Cunningham & Walsh [advertising agency] set up a panel of families who did not own television sets. At that time, a record was made of activities during evening hours. In 1951 these *same* families were again interviewed. A careful record was *again* made of what each individual was then doing on the average weekday evening. In order to measure change in social activity the records for the two years were compared.

Very little change in social activity was shown for the families in the panel who had *not* purchased television sets during the year. They were doing just about what they had been doing the year before.

In those panel families, who during the year had purchased a TV set, there was a marked change. Movie attendance had dropped 77 per cent; radio listening had dropped 88 per cent on the average weekday evening. Other changes were a 53 per cent drop in number of adults reading a magazine, an 87 per cent drop in entertaining, and a 74 per cent drop in visiting. The time devoted to TV viewing had encroached on almost every social activity during the evening hours.

The drop in entertaining is certainly contrary to what happened in 1948, 1949, and earlier when TV was very new. Then, ownership of a TV set meant a definite increase in entertaining— both invited and uninvited. During . . . [1950 and 1951] this aspect of TV has become less important. Too many families now have their own set.

. . . [In 1952] when these same families were called on for the third time, further decreases were noted in some activities. One exception is visiting, which went up 27 per cent but remained well below what it had been in pre-television days. Another exception is radio listening which increased slightly, due mostly to increased use of radio during early and late evening hours. The net result, after two years of TV ownership, is that other activities have dropped to about the level found in our random sample of families who have sets from under one to over five years old.

Apparently the major effect on other activities is experienced during the first year of set ownership. After that year other activities level off, moving up and down slightly each year, but continuing to have a much less important part in the individual's life than before TV. Of course, this applies only to weekday evenings. The Videotown study has not yet attempted to measure television's effect on Saturday and Sunday, and only to a moderate degree its effect during daytime hours. It is probably too early to forecast future trends since TV itself, both technically and artistically, is still developing. So far there is no indication of an inclination to resume many activities curtailed since TV became available.

The slight upswing in radio noted among families who purchased TV sets in 1951 is also noted in the random sample of all TV families. People in these families showed a 50 per cent increase . . . [in 1952] in number of people listening to radio at sometime during the evening. Again this increase occurred mostly during early and late evening hours.

During the daytime, radio listening has been less affected by TV, as might be expected at this early stage in the development of daytime TV. In TV homes, radio listening during morning hours in 1951 was at a higher level than in the non-TV homes (among women, of course). Afternoon listening was about 50 per cent lower in TV than in non-TV homes. . . . [In 1952] in both TV and non-TV homes, radio listening increased during the morning hours both for women and the family as a whole. Afternoon listening to radio increased in TV homes, remained about the same in non-TV homes.

Although TV viewing increased over . . . [1951] in both morning and afternoon, it is still only about one-third as high as radio listening in the morning. In the afternoon TV viewing grows gradually in importance; by 4 P.M., about the time the children get home from school, TV viewing jumps ahead of radio listening in TV homes.

During morning hours it was noted that radio listening was coincidental with some other activity in 75 per cent of the cases, usually some form of housework. One of the problems facing TV is that of making daytime programs as interesting to hear as they are to see.

Newspaper reading is just about the only regular activity which showed no change after the advent of TV. Among the group of families who purchased a TV set during 1951, newspaper reading actually increased 9 per cent that year. It increased another 20 per cent in 1952. This increase was not limited to the 1951 buyers of TV. It was noted in all groups of families. Among non-set-owners there was no increase in the number of people reading newspapers in 1951, but an increase of 40 per cent in 1952. In the random sample of all TV set owners, newspaper reading increased 40 per cent in 1951 and almost doubled in 1952. With these increases, the level of newspaper reading today is the same in TV families as in nonowner families on the average weekday evening. While figures are less exact on time spent, the indication is that there is very little difference between TV and non-TV homes. It is interesting to note that the wife usually reads her evening paper early in the afternoon (home delivery) or late in the evening. The husband apparently appropriates it when he gets home from work.

Inspection of hourly records of each person's activity quickly shows that TV has replaced these other pastimes. Between the hours of 5 and bedtime, which is usually between 11 and 12 o'clock (they are even staying up later this year), TV occupies an average of 2.33 hours per person. When they are at home and watching TV, the average is 3.25 hours per person, or about half of their evening hours. The set is tuned in an average of almost four hours an evening. Where the set is tuned in at all, the average is 4.5 hours. . . . The trend is toward a rotating family audience. Set hours are growing slightly faster than viewing hours per person. The set is on and the family comes and goes depending on interest in the program. Average hours of viewing, when watching at all, range from 2.41 hours per weekday evening for children under 10, to 3.52 for wives, 3.58 for husbands, and 3.83 for other adult males.

COMING UP: 2000 TV STATIONS [2]

The end of the Federal Communications Commission's freeze on new station construction will by no means solve all of . . . television's worries; in fact it gives rise to a new crop of problems and a host of possibilities.

The ban was imposed . . . [in 1948] when the FCC and the industry saw that use of the very high frequencies only would not permit adequate national television coverage. Before granting permits for further VHF [very high frequency] station construction, the FCC wanted to investigate expansion into the ultra-high frequencies. By using UHF's [ultra-high frequency] 70 channels in addition to VHF's 12, the United States could have some 2000 stations instead of the 400 possible with VHF alone.

At the time the freeze was clamped on, no one had any idea that it would last so long. In fact the industry kept prodding the

[2] From "What Does the End of the TV Freeze Mean?" by Victor J. Dallaire, Associate Editor, *Printers' Ink. Printers' Ink.* 239:29. April 4, 1952. Reprinted by permission. Copyright 1952 by Printers' Ink Pub. Co., Inc. 205 East 42d Street. New York 17, N. Y.

FCC to get it lifted. But it was a big job for the undermanned commission, Korea came along, and the color television controversy burned up at least a year of the commission's time.

As the freeze ends, this is the situation: There are 108 commercial operations on the air, most of them well into the black, thanks to the long period of grace the freeze gave them. But these 108 stations are not necessarily permanent fixtures. Some have requested power increases and other improvements. The FCC may switch some from one VHF channel to another, possibly from VHF to UHF. In addition, the commission has more than 500 applications for new stations on file and expects another 500 when it starts accepting them again after the waiting period during which prospective operators are supposed to study its allocations.

The end of the freeze doesn't mean that new stations will start breaking out all over. According to law, the FCC must hold a hearing on each application, and that takes time, since many applications are contested. Putting up a station and getting a station on the air takes more time. . . . Transmitting equipment is not considered an immediate problem—a special task force of the Radio and Television Manufacturers Association only recently reported that plenty of it was on hand to meet immediate needs, that the industry could produce it fast enough to meet foreseeable requirements under present critical materials allotments.

In handling applications, the FCC probably will deal first with cities of large size that have no television stations now, like Portland (Oregon) or Denver. Following them will come smaller cities with no TV, then large cities with only one . . . [television] station, Pittsburgh, for example. Finally, the commission will work on applications for UHF outlets from cities that already have their share of VHF stations. That's to be the order for the batch of applications on hand, at any event.

Eventually, some optimists say as soon as five years from now, television will blanket the country as radio does today with 2000 stations, 200 of which have been reserved for noncommercial users such as schools. Educational and cultural use of television has been a hot subject for the past few months, but at present only one application for a noncommercial franchise is on file.

At some time in the future, too, the nation's present television set owner population . . . will be more than doubled, but this isn't going to be a painless increase. Present sets can receive only VHF telecasts, and the bulk of the new stations, although not necessarily the first ones to be added, will be sending out a UHF signal. That means that converters must be added to existing sets, and new sets must be able to pick up both UHF and VHF. The converters will cost extra; the UHF-VHF receivers will cost more than the present sets.

The set makers, of course, are happy to see the end of the freeze. . . . There's no doubt that addition of new stations eventually will produce a demand for receivers similar to that of 1949. The transmitter equipment manufacturers, barring war, can expect a fine, healthy business for years to come.

The problems of the new stations are a little more complex. The UHF outlet owners are going to have to build an audience from scratch in most instances, but they should be able to profit from the experience of the VHF pioneers. They're bound to operate in the red for some time under the best of conditions; where they buck established VHF competition, it might be a lot longer than they bargain for.

New stations will strengthen present networks, probably bring some new ones. To the movie people, it'll probably mean another blow on the box office, increased emphasis on TV-film production and a renewed drive to get theatre-TV going. To radio it'll mean a tougher fight than it is currently waging for the advertising dollar and that even shorter commodity, talent.

The thaw isn't going to bother the advertiser to any great extent for at least a year. The addition of 20 or 30 stations won't result in any great budget or time-buying changes, but after that, when television becomes a national medium in its truest sense, it's bound to affect everybody connected with advertising. Just how is anybody's guess at the moment.

The end of the freeze then eventually will result in bringing television to practically everybody who wants it; it will bring about billions of dollars in set sales, at least $2 billion worth of transmitting equipment business. It will mean a good many changes in advertising, radio, publishing and the movies.

TELEVISION AND HOLLYWOOD [3]

According to Audience Research Inc., residents of homes with television sets recently listed their entertainment preferences as follows: 37 per cent favored television; 28 per cent movies; and 4 per cent radio.

As between TV and movies, "studies by various agencies including Audience Research have shown that the frequency of television set owners' motion-picture attendance is anywhere from 20 to 30 per cent below what it was before they acquired a set. . . . Unless the industry can win many of these television owners back to greater frequencies of movie attendance by the excellence of the entertainment offered, the effect will be a serious one."

If the Audience Research figures are correct, then the conclusion is an understatement. It takes more than "excellence" to recapture a lost audience. Hollywood knows this from experience, having weathered a similar though lesser crisis twenty years ago, with the coming of sound. The case is worth examining briefly, for it throws an instructive light upon the mutations of the mass media, as they occur within the structure of democratic-capitalistic society. It shows how majestic and irresistible is the march of technological progress, but it also reveals how very closely this movement is related to the profit motive—which, in turn, is geared to certain unpredictable urgencies of appetite and fashion among the masses for whose entertainment such media exist and upon whose favor such profits depend.

The Jazz Singer was made in 1927. Within a year there was not a silent picture in production in Hollywood.

It can be said, without reopening the old debate over the esthetic merits of silent versus sound film, that the first talkies of the late 1920's were inferior, in every respect but novelty, to the full-fledged silents which they supplanted. Yet the issue between them was never seriously in doubt.

[3] From "Battle over Television," by John Houseman, producer of plays, motion pictures, and radio programs. *Harper's Magazine.* 200:51-9. May 1950. Reprinted by permission.

Looking back, it is clear that the determining factor in this sweeping victory of sound film was not quality; it was the sudden, overwhelming excitement stirred up by the new dimension of sound. For the gratification of this added sense, audiences were willing, nay eager, to forgo the cinematic delights of speed and scope for whose sake, only a few years before, they had deserted the theatre for the movies.

But here is the most striking thing of all: This "revolutionary" invention of sound that altered the face of picture business *contained no single element, theoretical or practical, that had not been known and available to the industry for a generation or more.* Because there seemed to be no profit in it, financial or artistic, Hollywood ignored it; the public, unaware of its existence, remained uninterested. It took drastic economic pressure —months of steadily falling receipts, sagging audiences, and, finally, the sheer desperation of certain weak elements in the industry—to spur Hollywood into adopting this innovation, which the public then so instantly embraced. . . .

It is startling to discover how closely, and in how many respects, the parallel holds between the first months of talkies and the first years of television. The best of TV, as viewed in the American home today, is inferior in technical and artistic quality to the average movie being shown in the nation's 20,000 theatres. Its image is unsteady and blurred in texture, diminutive in size, and lacking balance or perspective between the visual and auditory elements presented. TV's general run of production, even by "B" picture standards, is poor, hurried, and inept, with the millstone of radio-thinking still heavy about its neck. In its choice and preparation of dramatic material, TV remains seriously limited by considerations of expense and copyright.

Yet we have seen that television's popularity as a form of entertainment, at the most conservative estimate, exceeds that of movies by one third and that of radio, for all its accumulation of stars and habit and good will, by almost 1000 per cent!

As in the case of the first talkies, the nature of this public enthusiasm is obvious. To American audiences, TV offers the lure of a new dimension. To a hundred million radio listeners, it brings the irresistible gift of sight. For fifty million movie-goers it means an end to the limitations of time and space; what formerly the patron had to go out and seek and pay for is now brought into his home by an obedient electrical genie, at the instant of its occurrence and absolutely free, or so it seems. It gets paid for, of course, just as surely as if the money were clicking through a till.

With one last item, the parallel is complete: This Magic Box that is now setting the communications world afire has been available, in roughly its present form, since the middle thirties. It has been held back for more than a dozen years, for the excellent reason that no one stood to profit by it and, therefore, nobody wanted it. The movie industry didn't, and still doesn't. Radio didn't. Why should it? Networks, advertising agencies, line-lessors, patent controllers, equipment manufacturers—why should any of these willingly disrupt the happy status quo which was capable of yielding an annual $2 billion in radio billings and the profits from the sale of seventeen million radio sets a year?

It was not until the saturation point for equipment finally seemed to have been reached, and business as a whole began to show definite signs of sagging, that the radio industry and the financial interests that control it, at long last, gave the go-ahead to the new medium, and opened the floodgates of a public enthusiasm that now threatens to modify the entire structure of the entertainment business.

With faith in our still expanding economy and in the miraculous powers of applied science, we may assume that, within a decade, TV will be a technically perfect instrument with almost universal coverage. This will make it, automatically, the dominant medium of mass communication in the world. As such, what will be its relationship to those other, older forms of communication and entertainment which it is destined to supplement or replace? (Its effect on the present system of publication does not concern us here, but it seems likely that many of the functions of the press will be taken over in due course by the Magic Box.)

The theatre has nothing to fear from the new competition— movies and radio having already done all the harm there is to be done in that department. Artistically, because home-viewed tele-

vision is a more intimate and probably more articulate dramatic
form than the full-screen movie, TV, whether it is produced
'live" or "canned," is likely to have a closer and more constructive association with the living theatre than any of the other mass
media have had to date.

Radio was never more than a transitional stage, a step towards
television. It is likely to continue fulfilling a useful, though
minor, function as a carrier of music and a disseminator of
cultural items not appreciably enhanced by the addition of sight.
In the major fields of entertainment, including news and drama,
radio is almost certainly a dead duck.

Motion pictures and television are the great and bitter rivals
of the future, according to general belief. Actually, they are not
competitors at all but variants of the same medium. (In both,
an action or the imitation of an action is electrically projected
upon a luminous screen—directly, in one case; in the other,
remotely.) The coming struggle for power is not between movies
and TV as forms of entertainment and communication, but between the rival systems already set up for their exploitation.

In this struggle, two great empires stand opposed. On the
one side is picture business, with its $2.5 billion investment in
theatres, its tributary production industry, and its seventy million
weekly patrons. On the other is radio—a $4.5 billion structure of
four major networks, two thousand stations, . . . and an estimated
150 million listening hours a day.

These are the giants locked in combat for the favor of the
public. They are fighting to retain, and if possible increase, the
huge profits they have been making for so many years by such
radically different methods: movies, by direct levy, at the box
office; radio, through commercial advertising, by indirect levy
upon the American people.

Ask a radio man about TV. You will find that he regards it
as his own legitimate territory, by right of direct succession. He
is convinced that television, in its general lines, will follow the
existing pattern of commercial radio, with certain inevitable
changes in production methods to suit the new medium.

Ask a motion-picture man, an exhibitor. Unless he is deluding himself, he will not try to minimize the technical wonders of television. He will tell you that while home-viewing has its place in the family life of the future, the gregarious instinct which from time immemorial has driven men to gather in crowds in a common meeting place will insure the continued patronage of the nation's twenty thousand theatres—whose air-conditioning plants, as one observer puts it, "can be credited with attracting almost as many people as the pictures on the screen." The local pleasure palace will remain, according to this view, the favorite haunt and focal point of the community. Here, finer entertainment will be offered than ever before. In countless theatres equipped with TV projection, the audience of the future will be treated to the best of the Hollywood product spiced with sports, news events, and famous vaudeville acts televised at the instant of their occurrence.

One enterprising showman in the state of California has made his own original contribution to the debate. He has hired a small, abandoned movie theatre, moved the seats around, installed TV, and opened his doors for business. When it was pointed out to him that he could not legally charge the public for admission to an entertainment which he, himself, was receiving free, he replied that such was not his intention. His profits would be made, he declared, from the sale of popcorn, soft drinks, and candy!

From barroom to soft-drink parlor is a natural step; the free public enjoyment of televised entertainment is likely to play an ever-increasing part in the crowd habits of the future. But, as a practical matter, it is between home-viewing and theatre exhibition, as the dominant method of picture exploitation, that the heat of the battle rages and will continue to rage for some time to come. To predict at this time the decisive triumph of one or the other would obviously be absurd; though, even now, evidence exists which suggests that the attractions of home-viewing definitely outweigh the gregarious urge among the mass of the population. . . .

This is not to say that tall grass will shortly be growing amidst the ruins of Rialtos, Criterions, Granadas, and other abandoned Main Street landmarks from coast to coast. It does suggest, quite emphatically, that in seeking customers for his product, the picture-maker of the future cannot afford to overlook the vast new home audience suddenly made available through the technical wonders of television. It is not generally realized how very limited was the maximum coverage of the movie theatres even at the peak of their prosperity. Today, out of 110 million potential customers in the United States, not more than 13 per cent ever get to see the average picture. It is any wonder that the movie industry (that section of it that is not primarily concerned with protecting its investments in theatrical real estate) is greatly excited at the idea of such a possible expansion in distribution? Is it surprising that Hollywood should look forward, eagerly, to the day when its creations will be available to the public, no longer in the comparative restriction of twenty thousand theatres, but on the private screens of fifty million American homes?

This is a thrilling prospect—one that will probably be realized in our time. But there are obvious obstacles to be overcome and one very vexing question, to which, at the moment, there is no easy answer: *Who pays?* We have no merchandising method in this country that even suggests a solution; there is no available mechanism by which a home audience may, at present, pay for its chosen entertainment.[4]

It goes even deeper than that. The very notion of a paying audience runs counter to the established principles of the radio industry, over whose existing facilities this entertainment is going to travel. For twenty years, the radio audience has been receiving its shows absolutely free; the theory being that, in due course, it will purchase, or cause others to purchase, the products which it has heard advertised, in sufficient quantity to justify a continuation of the free show. The system has worked, apparently, to the general satisfaction. Whenever payment for radio entertainment has been suggested, in the form of license fees or through direct charges, it has been violently rejected by the industry and the public alike.

[4] However, see selection "Pay as You Look," p25-30.—Ed.

But now things are changing. As radio emerges from its blindness, through television, and enters into direct competition with the current motion-picture product, it is unlikely that audiences will long be satisfied with a double standard of entertainment quality. Today, the ratio of production cost, as between one minute of Hollywood feature film and one minute of top dramatic TV, is roughly twenty to one. Expanding television markets may modify this proportion, but there is a ceiling of cost beyond which the advertiser, for obvious reasons, cannot be expected to go. While money does not necessarily spell quality, audiences have learned to expect, and will not lightly surrender, certain standards of luxury in their visual entertainment which the radio industry, as presently constituted, simply cannot afford to supply.

There are two alternatives: either the standards of entertainment must be lowered, or new methods must be found to exploit, through the medium of television, not only "the greatest concentration of talent in the entertainment world" but also the American public's demonstrated willingness, under the right conditions, to pay for the product of this talent to the tune of billions of dollars a year.

Our social and economic structure is not so rigid that such a mutually desirable alliance cannot be arranged. It is a matter of finding means, technical and economic, whereby two such radically different types—the sponsor-selected show that comes free and the freely-selected show that must be paid for—can be married and live in harmony on the American air waves. . . .

It is too early yet to define the exact shape of things to come among the mass media. Whatever happens, it will not be without blood, sweat, and tears. These will be shed, respectively, by the business men struggling to control this expansion and harness it for profit; by the engineers, for whom the conquest of the horizon through the coaxial cable and the practical transmission of a colored image are only the first of many obstacles to be overcome; and finally, I suspect, by the psychologists and the sociologists, concerned with the mental health of a generation that is living ever less in the realities of personal experience, more and more by remote observation and through vicarious emotion.

THEATRE TELEVISION [5]

Television . . . is in the process of forming a strong and permanent alliance with its most formidable competitor, the motion picture theatre. . . .

There is nothing Buck Rogerish about a prediction that in the not too distant future there will be hundreds and possibly thousands of movie houses linked together into regional and national networks to carry televised shows simultaneously on their screens. Their programs, unavailable in the home, will be in color as well as black and white. This is theatre television. . . .

The extent to which this will change the broadcast pattern is anybody's guess. Under the present circumstances, with the TV audiences increasingly fed up with the repetitive and limited program fare going out over the air, even the staunchest supporters of the status quo are loath to deny that television badly needs a new source of revenue if its entertainment content is to keep pace with its formal physical expansion and technical progress.

Proponents of theatre television confidently predict that, once enough [movie] houses are equipped with large-screen TV facilities, they will be able to bring their audiences the best in televised operas, concerts, plays, musicals, sports events and other events of a quality which home TV so far has been unable to attain. . . .

The prime obstacle is one of economics. Although visual in its appeal, television has been reared in the traditions of commercial radio. It is gradually and painfully dawning on the broadcasters that the electronic twins may not be identical after all. TV is acknowledged as the perfect advertising medium, but sponsors are left goggle-eyed when faced with the astronomical rise in costs which has all but eliminated any incentive for trying experimental shows. Much of what logically should be TV material, such as quality films produced especially with video requirements in mind, has never been within the economic reach of the sponsors.

[5] From "Pay as You View TV," by Fred Hift, staff member of motion picture trade publication. *Theatre Arts*. 36:26-8. April 1952. Reprinted by permission.

And it was perhaps inevitable that the motion picture/theatres should sooner or later meet the TV challenge of television with the realistic attitude that "If you can't lick 'em, join 'em."

Theatre television, which harnesses the instantaneous quality of television and combines it with the scope and depth of the movie screen, is accomplished in two basic ways.

In one, the "instantaneous projection" method, the television picture is projected to the screen through a system of mirrors. This gives viewers the impression of having a front-row seat at an event that is unfolding at the very moment at some other place and carries with it the excitement of the unexpected.

The second, or "film recording" method, involves the photographing of the image from the face of the TV tube. The resultant film is developed, processed, and can be thrown on the screen within as little as twenty seconds. The advantage of this system is that it permits delayed presentation, repeat performances and possible editing out of slow or undesirable sequences.

Although large-screen television has stepped out of the laboratory only fairly recently, it has already been shown in brilliant color. . . . [In 1951 the Radio Corporation of America] put on a full-scale demonstration of instantaneous projection color theatre TV. At the moment the government has clamped down on the production of all color receivers, but exhibitors are pressing for exemption from the order, raising the distinct possibility that color television may come to the movie theatres before it arrives in the home.

Theoretically at least, the possibilities of theatre television are limited only by the economic power which the nation's . . . theatres can generate among themselves. Much depends on the attitude of the Federal Communications Commission which is currently investigating not only the possibility of allocating special channels to the film houses but also the desirability of having the theatres run such an exclusive television service in the first place. In an elementary and experimental way theatre TV has already given an inkling of its ultimate capabilities. Some seventy motion picture houses . . . [as of early 1952 were] already equipped to carry it and most of them can be linked together into a network. . . . They [have] managed to capture some important boxing matches from home television, much to the annoyance of those who counted on the implied promise of "free" entertainment when they bought their sets. The fight fans, grumbling at not being able to tune in on the event at home but unwilling to miss it altogether, plunked down their dollars at the theatre box office. Once the bout was under way, the movie house became a noisy arena, and near-riot resulted in one theatre when the equipment broke down temporarily.

A number of houses also tried televised accounts of the Kefauver hearings and General MacArthur's home-coming. Others offered baseball, football and other sports, but the most successful attractions were always the ones which the theatres had all to themselves. Once the legend "Television Tonight" becomes a regular fixture on the marquees of several thousand theatres, large-screen video can become serious competition for the home telecasters, bidding vigorously for exclusive rights to big events.

Once again, the economics of television favor the theatres. Where a producer today cannot afford to let his play go on local television without risking a debacle at the box office, the movie theatres could offer him a very different and much more attractive proposition. Once the production opens on Broadway and wins critical acclaim, that same week, hundreds of other theatres throughout the country could show a televised version of that same play, with the original cast. New York houses would of course refrain from joining in, and the producer's box office would be greatly enlarged by his share in the out-of-town receipts. Theatre TV enthusiasts maintain this could not only do away with the risky practice of sending out road shows but could bring Broadway to Mainstreets still untouched by the road companies.

Joseph H. McConnell, president of the National Broadcasting Company, recently anticipated that 4000 or more theatres would be television-equipped by 1955. The blueprints make provision for centrally located studios from where the shows can be piped to the theatres. On the West Coast a group of theatres already have entered serious discussions for the televising of *South Pacific;* the Theatre Guild has displayed lively interest in offering a series of plays for exclusive telecasting to the theatres. . . . [The Metropolitan Opera recently performed "Carmen" through TV for the movie houses—Ed.]

The whole plan, unfortunately, hinges to a considerable extent on the theatres' ability to qualify for exclusive channels from the FCC. Although they deny it, they have been charged with a plot to monopolize good TV programs for their own use by virtue of their economic power and such accusations do not sit well with the competition-minded FCC. . . .

It can reasonably be assumed that . . . theatre television . . . will eventually go into full-scale operation. . . . [Its] success will depend on whether the spectator is willing to pay his way rather than let the advertising sponsor pay it for him. There is also reason to believe he is.

PAY AS YOU LOOK [6]

It could have been a Saturday matinee at the neighborhood movie palace. The kids yowled and fought and ran among the chairs. They scrapped for better seats and then did not sit in them. Not even Ed Burns could do anything with them and he is a big and burly Chicago cop. The children just could not wait for the movie to begin.

At last it was time. . . . Mrs. Burns went to the telephone while her husband switched on the television receiver. Vainly he shushed the kids so that Mrs. Burns could hear.

"Phonevision operator?" she asked. "We would like to see *Welcome Stranger,* please."

The rest of her conversation was drowned out by the screaming children. The television screen had suddenly come alive. It blossomed into lights, skittery figures, planes of weird shadows. The images jiggled back and forth on the screen. They wouldn't stay still. Apparently, the transmitter had the shakes.

Then, in one breath-taking instant, all the movement stopped and there was a clear, quiet test pattern. Ed Burns had tuned in the scrambled image from the phonevision station and Mrs.

[6] From "What About Pay-as-You-Look TV?" by Victor Ullman, writer. *Saturday Evening Post.* 224:30+. August 25, 1952. Reprinted by permission.

Burns, by making a telephone call, had unscrambled it. Along miles of telephone lines from downtown Chicago, an electric impulse was sent right into the Burns television set to stop the jitter of the signal sent over the air.

There was comparative quiet when the announcer began. They were watching experimental phonevision station KS2XBS, the first of its kind, owned and operated by the Zenith Radio Corporation by permission of the Federal Communications Commission. This was the last day, the announcer continued, of a ninety-day test of phonevision. The movie to be presented immediately was *Welcome Stranger,* starring Bing Crosby and Barry Fitzgerald. Later in the evening, at 9:30, the 300 Chicago families participating in the test could view *The Hucksters* with Clark Gable.

The title flashed on and the opening music began. . . .

For an hour and forty-seven minutes the fanciful tale unfolded. The story was not interrupted by television commercials. The pictures were crystal-clear. Subtle lighting and photography reflected all the clean vistas of the little New England town. When Bing bickered with Barry or pursued his musical wooing of Joan Caulfield, his voice remained consistent in tone and volume. There were none of the fade-ins and fade-outs of the moving TV microphones on live shows, none of the muddiness of Kinescope.

The whole presentation was in the companionable atmosphere of a movie theatre, except that the "theatre" was transferred to the Burns living room and it cost Ed Burns one dollar.

Much has been said about phonevision, but its most important aspect is that it allowed Mrs. Burns to raise the telephone and "order" a Hollywood movie for her own home. Everything else about phonevision is incidental. . . .

Every [American television screen] . . . is a pipe line to the world. It can, and, on occasion, has become the stage of the Metropolitan Opera in New York; the United States Senate gallery; an office window on Canal Street during the New Orleans Mardi Gras; the operating amphitheatre of the Mayo Clinic; Ebbets Field or Soldier Field; Madison Square Garden or Saint

Patrick's Cathedral. Wherever a TV camera can go, Ed Burns' living room can follow.

But for purely theatrical entertainment, the camera can go only where someone has paid the price of admission—and that's the rub. For a generation of radio, advertising has paid the bills for entertainment over the air. Advertising has paid for its own sponsored programs and, as the sole support of the broadcasting industry, has made it possible for stations and networks to donate time for the civic and public-service programs which give valuable communication to the Red Cross, the American Cancer Society, the host of other organizations engaged in humanitarian work.

Came television and its economic headaches. Program costs have reached staggering figures. Although the number of TV sponsors is growing by leaps and bounds, costs continue to go up by even longer leaps and bigger bounds; there's a limit to every advertising budget.

It is in this economic climate that pay-as-you-see television enters the scene. Phonevision, sponsored by Zenith; Telemeter, sponsored by Paramount Pictures, and the new Skiatron device are variations of this idea, which would survive by extracting fees from television viewers instead of sponsors.

Only phonevision has been tested to date. The FCC authorized its Chicago test in order to determine whether or not the American people will break a tradition of free entertainment over the air and will buy entertainment that television cannot bring them. In the 1920's there had been efforts to establish subscription radio, but they failed. Free entertainment over the air was too good and it satisfied the people.

Now, however, something new has been added. We are all accustomed to paying for visual entertainment and some of the top men in amusement believe that a home "box-office" is inevitable. Paul Raibourn, of Paramount Pictures, . . . is very positive about it. He says "There will be some form of subscription television within five years."

If the reports from the Chicago test of phonevision are a criterion, Raibourn may be wrong only in timing.

From outright opposition . . . , the production side of the movie industry has turned to careful cooperation with development of a pay-as-you-see system. From outright refusal to allow their movies to be shown over phonevision, until the big stick of antitrust action was mentioned, a few of the major producers today keep some of their films in Chicago vaults for the exclusive use of phonevision demonstrations.

The reasons for this reversal are in the results of the Chicago test which ended on March 31, [1951]. . . .

The Zenith Radio Corporation spent more than $600,000 on the phonevision test. This included the installation of a special transmitter purchased from the General Electric Company in Syracuse, New York; a special switchboard installed in the downtown exchange of the Illinois Bell Telephone Company; television sets for each of the 300 homes, whether they had one or not, and equipping them for phonevision.

For ninety days and nights this highly exclusive audience had the choice of going out to the neighborhood movie palace, watching ordinary television, listening to radio, reading a book, attending a sports event or throwing a party. But they had an additional choice. They could buy, at a cost of one dollar, the movie phonecast for them alone.

Not one of the ninety films shown was a new, first-run production. The newest was released in September 1948, and some were more than ten years old. Yet during the test, attendance at the ''Phonevision Theatre'' was at a ratio of more than $3\frac{1}{2}$ times the average weekly attendance at movie theatres throughout the country! The phonevision families bought 1.73 movies a week while the country average is .47 movies a week. This comparison, of course, is misleading, because it accounts only for an urban population, where movie facilities and habits are well developed. One family attended phonevision seventy-four times in the ninety days. That is an expenditure of $74. Another family bought just two phonecasts throughout the test period.

But the factor that made the movie people stop, look and count was the discovery of a gold mine in subscription television. All the ninety pictures shown had been through the movie mill, from first to second to third-run theatres. Yet only about 20 per

39058

cent of the potential phonevision audience had ever seen them before!

Mr. and Mrs. Gabriel Andreozzi, of North Ashland Avenue, Chicago, were selected for the test. Mr. Andreozzi works as a custodian at a National Guard armory. The Andreozzis had attended exactly three movies since 1945, until phonevision was presented to them. The two elderly roomers in their house could not remember when they had last seen a movie. Yet the four members of this household bought thirty-one movies over phonevision, approximately ten a month.

This experience was repeated in dozens of families. Folks who never went to the movies, could not go or sought some other form of entertainment, now bought movies at home. The Burns children continued their attendance at the Saturday matinee because it is a social event they would never miss.

But Mrs. John Hagey, of West Barry Avenue, who loves movies, could go to them only occasionally, because of illness. She had her phonevision set installed in her bedroom so that she could watch phonevision while still obeying the doctor's orders. Until she went to the hospital early in March, Mrs. Hagey and her two maids bought phonevision almost nightly. . . .

What phonevision can mean to the sick, aged and sitterless families is obvious. What it can mean to the sick movie industry now losing some of its audiences to television is astounding.

Tracing through the financial fortunes of Paramount's *Welcome Stranger* we find that this picture grossed $6.1 million for its producers over a period of years. This was a highly successful production.

If the country's . . . television sets were now hooked up with phonevision, which grants 50 per cent of the income to producers, the phonevision test points to some startling potentialities. Suppose the same proportion of families owning TV sets bought *Welcome Stranger* as did the phonevision guinea pigs. In just three performances the producers would receive $2,985,-000. This, of course, is an optimistic projection. But even if only half the audience bought the picture, or 10 per cent of them, it still would represent a bonanza for the movies, because

Paramount carries *Welcome Stranger* on its books at a value of one dollar. They had thought it had been fully exploited.

No wonder the movies now are digging down in the vaults for films for TV as well as phonevision. The pictures considered "dead" and held by the major producers for years, at an investment of approximately $5 billion, have not been seen by about 80 per cent of the population. . . .

It must be remembered that phonevision could broadcast directly from the ring or athletic field, just as television does, but to a paying audience. It need not depend on movie films exclusively. Promoters of other sports spectacles, both amateur and professional, have also been impressed by the promise of phonevision. . . .

The phonevision test proved that these pay-as-you-see gadgets are not a substitute for the movies, sports events or television. They are an addition to all of them. The American public would always be free to choose any form of entertainment desired, with or without phonevision. But the battle for FCC approval will be well worth watching.

TELEVISION AND SPORTS [7]

To the average sports promoter, the words "box office" can be freely translated into "bread and butter." Regardless of other sources of income that his event may generate, he feels that the backbone of his market has always been the people who pay to come and watch his contests. As a result, he is instinctively opposed to anything that tends to keep them away.

And in recent years, he has meant only one thing by "anything"—television. Whenever the gate falls off at any sports event, television gets the full blame, even if that event wasn't televised. The promoter figures that some other event was being aired, and people stayed home to watch it instead of coming to see his.

The only trouble with this theory is that it won't always hold up in practice. The figures show that in many cases televised

[7] From "Does Television Really Spoil the Gate?" *Business Week.* p38+. September 27, 1952. Reprinted by permission.

games do as well as or better than nontelevised games. . . . In fact, there's some indication that if television hadn't created new fans, some teams in some sports would be worse off than they are. . . .

Baseball: On the major-league baseball front, several important changes in TV plans for 1953 . . . [are] in the cards. The first of these was an announcement by the Washington Senators that it would drop all telecasts of its home games—despite the fact that through Labor Day the club was about 12,000 tickets ahead of 1951 sales on a comparable date. President Clark Griffith stated that he felt that TV was a definite threat to the box office at home games. So in its place, he hopes to televise only the Senators' road games.

President Dan Topping of the New York Yankees would like to do the same thing. And he has better reason: Whereas the Yankees for several past seasons have hit or barely missed the 2 million attendance figure, . . . [in 1952] they . . . [were] lucky to wind up with 1.6 million. But Topping can't arbitrarily drop home-game TV in favor of road TV only. He must first get the other two New York clubs—the Brooklyn Dodgers and the New York Giants—to agree to follow the same policies. Otherwise, Topping's telecasts of road games would conflict with their home-game telecasts—and scramble the whole elaborate schedule the clubs have set up to avoid conflicts. . . .

Mediocre attendance wasn't limited to the New York teams. Baseball as a whole was off 9 per cent through Labor Day, as compared with . . . [1951's] attendance. Yet right here you get the first factor which throws off the calculations on the effect of TV: Four of the 16 major-league teams . . . exceeded their total 1951 gate by September 1. . . . All four televise at least some home games.

A closer study made at the end of last season brought forth some even more disturbing factors. Jerry Jordan, youthful independent researcher who is strongly in favor of televising sports, analyzed the nine baseball teams which had maintained their regular televising of at least all home daytime games. He found that they had played to an increase of 234,169 people in the park in 1951 over 1950. On the other hand, the seven which reduced, restricted, or eliminated TV in 1951 suffered an aggregate loss of 1.4 million.

But as in the case of all statistics, there's a catch here which the figures fail to show. And that is that the ball teams with the heaviest TV schedules also had the best performances.

Football: In 1951, the National Collegiate Athletic Association had set up a program of restricted telecasts, under which only one game would be telecast in a given area each Saturday. . . . NCAA announced that its purpose was "experimental," designed to study the effect of limited or blacked-out Saturdays on gate receipts. Most objective observers felt that the plan proved nothing at all, one way or the other. For one thing, overall college football attendance was down 6 per cent in 1951 from 1950. For another, according to Jerry Jordan, colleges in TV areas reported a loss of only 4 per cent, while those in non-TV areas were down 10 per cent.

Perhaps because of these factors, NCAA . . . [ignored] the box office study approach . . . [in 1952]; it hasn't even mentioned it as a reason for continuing limitations. Instead, it said that the aim of the 1952 plan is to prevent monopolization of TV revenue by a few big schools. So, in the 11-game schedule, no school may be televised more than once, giving 22 colleges a slice of the TV pie. . . .

Boxing: The professional boxing business is hard at work trying to figure out the most profitable kind of television. The International Boxing Club, leading promoter of bouts, has a strong reluctance against network TV when it comes to outstanding fights. As a result, the public is getting ever fewer chances to see the really big fights in its own living room. . . .

One . . . example of this trend came . . . in the Joe Walcott-Rocky Marciano fight for the world's heavyweight championship. Held in Philadelphia, the fight went out on a closed network to about 50 theatres all over the country.

The theatre network has been set up by Theater Network Television, Inc. According to rumor, TNT is paying IBC about $1 for each ticket sold by the theatres in the lineup, with a minimum of about $140,000 guaranteed. The theatres themselves are selling tickets ranging in price from $3.60 to $4.80.

Yet the advantages of controlled television have not blinded promoters completely to the advantages of sponsored network TV. In fact, there is some mighty fancy money available for network television from sponsors only too eager to pay it because sports programs are surefire audience getters. IBC, for example, has signed a new $4 million contract with Pabst Brewing Co. to telecast its Wednesday night bouts for the next 52 weeks. General Motors has signed to spend more than $2.6 million for the privilege of sponsoring the 11 college games being telecast this fall.

And professional baseball, worrying about falling gates, nevertheless took in more than $4.5-million from TV in 1951.

TELEVISION IN PUBLIC LIFE

EDITOR'S INTRODUCTION

The presidential election campaign of 1952 was literally brought home to millions of American families. Responsible for this was television—which put on display for a nation-wide gallery of spectators virtually every detail from nominating conventions to the inauguration ceremony.

Many people believe that television, its hold on political campaigning secured, should now move into the field of legislation, investigation, and legal proceedings. Others, however, point to counterbalancing dangers. This section assesses the role of television in public life today, and includes differing views on its further extension in this field.

THE CHANGED LOOK IN POLITICAL CAMPAIGNING [1]

The experts will [long] be calculating the extent to which television helped to elect the . . . [new] President of the United States. Armed with slide-rules, past statistics, and comparative voting records for areas with and without TV, they will come up with judgments on the role of the new medium in its first big year in politics. . . .

Of the $30 million which, by the most modest estimates, the two major parties . . . [sank] into the [1952] campaign . . . more than one fourth . . . [was] spent on radio and TV. This does not count, of course, the roughly $8 million paid to the networks by commercial enterprises—Westinghouse, Philco and Admiral—for sponsoring TV coverage of the party conventions and of election-night returns. Nor does it include money spent for Pick the Winner, Meet the Press, Keep Posted, and other

[1] From "How Much Has TV Changed Campaigning?" by Robert Bendiner, writer on political affairs. New York *Times Magazine*. p 18+. November 2, 1952. Reprinted by permission.

commercially sponsored shows on which the issues of the campaign have been ventilated.

On this financial score alone the coming of TV has altered the normal course of campaigning. Even with all the generous loopholes in the Federal Corrupt Practices Act and the Hatch Act, there are limits to the amount of money that can be poured into a campaign. With a half-hour on a single television network running from $50,000 to $60,000, and even a twenty-second spot announcement coming to $600, it has been necessary to divert funds from more traditional campaign investments, such as billboards, advertising and even, to some extent, travel. . . .

Have the . . . [results been good] enough to warrant the huge expenditures and the feverish effort? Yes and no. Probably TV can be credited, using the word in terms of effectiveness, with at least three major campaign achievements. . . .

First, it enabled Adlai Stevenson, until the eve of the Democratic convention virtually the Great Unknown of American politics, to establish himself in three months as a figure of authentic stature. Politics aside, his eloquence, wit and unique personality, all conceded by the opposition, were impressed on the country to an extent that would hardly have been possible in so short a time by any other means, radio included.

Second, television must be rated a major factor in the remarkable comeback of [Vice President] Richard Nixon after revelations concerning his private finances seriously threatened to force him off the Republican ticket. Radio alone might have saved the day for Nixon, but there is no question that he proved himself a master of television technique and that the new medium counted very heavily in his rescue from impending disaster.

Third, though there is no way of proving it, television should probably be given a good share of credit for the unexpectedly high registration throughout the country. Not only did TV indirectly stimulate a big turnout by the political interest it aroused, but, along with radio, it very directly pounded away at the theme through spot announcements, "Get Out the Vote" shows, and other devices. The . . . campaign put on by WGAR of Cleveland, for example, has been credited with a 30 per cent registration increase in that area.

Nevertheless, there is a feeling in both radio-TV and political circles that television has not yet played, if indeed it ever will, the decisive campaign role that some enthusiasts predicted for it. . . .

The fact appears to be that far too much was expected of an untried and still experimental medium, and inevitably it fell short. At its peak of interest the Republican Convention earned a Hooper rating of 36 in New York City, as compared say, with the 62 recorded for "I Love Lucy," which just might have been a more diverting show. In their drearier stretches the conventions naturally rated far worse, dropping to a low of 17. What is even more to the point, reliable estimates indicate that in October, with the campaign reaching a crescendo, only 10 to 15 per cent of the people were even listening to the radio and TV speeches of the major presidential candidates. . . .

Even when the techniques of television are perfected, there is good reason to hope and assume it will never monopolize campaigning to the point of eliminating the grand tour, with all its old-fashioned fevers and follies. For, granting the powerful advantages television has already introduced, it has also brought with it exceedingly tricky problems.

Foremost among these is the obvious danger involved in this costliest of all types of campaigning. Government-imposed ceilings on expenditures, which meant little enough before, owing to gaps in the law, are now wholly absurd. Theoretically a national committee is limited to an outlay of $3 million, for an entire campaign. . . . Congress can raise the ceilings, of course, but what can it do to assure an equitable balance of expenditures . . . between two parties of unequal resources, not to mention the hardship that would be worked on a new party just coming into being?

Paul Porter, former chairman of the Federal Communications Commission, was recently moved to advise the networks that by allowing one party to dominate the airwaves in the closing days of the campaign, simply because it had the money to pay for it, they would invite "legislative reprisal." And Governor Stevenson himself has warned that "The problem of financing these costly campaigns presents to political parties the temptation to concentrate on large donations from a few individuals or private interests, which does not always serve the public interest best."

Private sponsorship of such public affairs as the Presidential conventions and election returns is another delicate problem raised by TV. Why, it has reasonably been asked, should a voter's most pressing business be brought to him, over his own airwaves, by courtesy of Westinghouse, or Philco, or Admiral? This mixing of business and politics is clearly hazardous, but if private sponsors don't foot the bill, who will? For all the $7.75 million paid out by these three corporations, the networks are still believed to have lost $2 million on the deal.

Obviously such problems as these will be intensified to the degree that television tends to replace other forms of campaigning. But there are factors other than financial that serve to keep any such tendency in check.

Repetition, for example, is the life of politics, as it is of advertising, but it makes extremely poor television. If you happen to be at the railroad station when your candidate's train stops at Wappingers Falls, you expect to hear from him the same catchwords and stock arguments you have already absorbed from your newspaper reading, from billboards, and from campaign literature. The chances are that you don't resent hearing them again.

But if, on your TV screen, you should subsequently hear and see your candidate put on precisely the same show at Yaphank, Owl's Head and East Sciatica—with the same trumped-up air of spontaneity—your enthusiasm would chill in short order. On the other hand, if you were to watch him change his tune from one section of the country, to another, your enthusiasm would chill even faster. None of this seamier aspect of campaigning is suitable to television.

With its constant demand for freshness, TV poses for politicians the same problem it poses for the entertainer. It consumes material at a prohibitive rate. If it were ever to replace the traditional forms of campaigning, a candidate would either require a regiment of speech writers or he would have to limit his campaign to something like a month—which might be a good idea at that.

The fireside type of television campaign presents a danger all its own. At first glance nothing could be more democratic than this direct contact between a candidate and his television audience, with no distracting scene stealers and no audience to sway the viewer with either partisan applause or catcalls. Perhaps it is the most satisfactory way of presenting a political argument, but if it is allowed to stand alone, without the wholesome questioning of the press or the chance of heckling, it can be an invitation to the demagogue. . . .

To cite these hazards and shortcomings of television as a political instrument is simply to suggest that, in spite of its enthusiasts, it is neither qualified nor destined to replace the traditional forms of American electioneering and its active reporting by a vigilant press. As an adjunct to these, however, it is already extremely valuable and will doubtless become more so.

Given a role in keeping with its power, its nature, and its demands, TV can serve to distill the essentials of campaign debate from the mass of flummery and empty rhetoric. It can establish a greater rapport between the nation and its potential leaders. It can arouse and sustain a wholesome public interest in the public business. And it can give a democracy a more intimate feel for its political machinery than it can hope to get from years of civics courses in school or from a desultory reading of the daily paper. All of which should provide justification enough, reward enough and glory enough for any institution.

CAN OUR POLITICAL SYSTEM SURVIVE TV? [2]

What TV is going to do to the tribal rites of American politics I still do not know. But I do know what TV coverage of the two [1952] national conventions has done to me: it . . . kept me for ten days enthralled, to my growing but helpless anger, by a spectacle of immense force and profound vulgarity. One particular shot that seems to have escaped the attention of

    [2] From "TV Coverage of National Conventions," by William S. Schlamm, staff writer. *Freeman.* 2:810. August 25, 1952. Reprinted by permission.

other critics, but will remain unforgettable for me, may explain my morose hunch that TV's impact on America's political future will be as degrading as it is inexorable.

A minister was giving the nightly invocation, and the TV camera was conveying the sudden hush of reverence even ward captains sense when the Lord is invoked. But then, just as ceremonial mention was made of Love, the cameraman took the cue and, whoosh, switched to a young lady in the aisle who was indeed a peach. . . .

The incident . . . identified, with an almost disarming frankness, the inherent nature of the medium. TV has unlimited means of reference, but its formative instinct is "entertainment"; and so it can not help being vulgar. It must vulgarize what it touches. And though only a few years ago such a feat would have been deemed hardly possible, it will succeed in degrading even politics. The two conventions have shown, at least to me, that this country tends to deteriorate into a government of, by and for the entertainment industry. True, TV will take you to the innermost councils of national politics but they will no longer be worth a look.

The entertainment industry proudly boasts that already its staggering power . . . determined the . . . [1952] convention results . . . .

Congratulating itself on such a stunning victory, the press (and by "press" I mean, in this era of modern communications, televised as well as printed journalism) has claimed that it functioned merely as the faithful guardian of the people's right to impose the popular will on party councils. . . . I challenge this presumption on two grounds.

One, the contention that the constitutional freedom of the press was involved is sheer hokum. The press has the constitutional right to publish all the information it can gather, but every citizen has the equally privileged right to release only so much information as suits him. TV had no more right to sit in on meetings of Republican committees than I have to sit in on policy conferences of the Columbia Broadcasting System's Board of Directors. If . . . [the broadcasters] wanted to expose some alleged machinations inside the Republican party, they were perfectly free to employ all the sleuthing ingenuity at their command. But TV's claim that its presence at private meetings of party groups was granted by the Bill of Rights is plainly insolent.

Secondly, our political system, to function properly, needs effectively organized and sovereign political parties. But to be sovereign, and effective to boot, a political party must retain its right to privacy and, yes, secrecy. To equate that secrecy of party council with rascality is the sort of fatuousness the vulgarians of the press so characteristically misrepresent as sophistication. The American political system—and few of its aspects are more admirable—distrusts "ideological" clashes and frankly favors the skillful compromise. This entirely honest, entirely legitimate principle of "deals" requires that intraparty conflicts be handled with a delicate concern for delicate stresses. It requires that artful professionals resolve intraparty tensions undisturbed by a gallery of millions—and this is nothing to be ashamed of.

The trustees of a party's sovereignty must be able to determine their party's moves as they see fit, and with the freedom of argument that comes only with privacy of council. This includes their license to make mistakes for which, if such mistakes are serious enough, they will duly forfeit their political lives. The untrammeled right to political failure is just as indispensable to free politics as the right to private bankruptcy is inseparable from free enterprise.

To exercise a political party's sovereignty is difficult enough in a nation whose regional, social and racial diversities make every political move a veritable adventure in tight-rope walking. It is altogether impossible when the mass-communications boys noisily take over. Their voices are amplified in inverse proportion to their ability to comprehend a tense situation in its subtle context. If permitted to prevail, their urge to turn politics into brassy entertainment is bound to kill both entertainment and politics. And while, if I had to, I could manage to live without the American entertainment industry, I do not care to survive the American political system.

HAZARDS OF POLITICAL BROADCASTING [3]

Every businessman regards himself, with some justice, as a connoisseur of weird government regulations. But among all the much-regulated businessmen of the United States, it is doubtful whether any are saddled with a more maddening set of rules than those governing the election-year behavior of radio and television stations. . . .

In every campaign the broadcaster risks lawsuits, serious trouble with the government, and serious trouble with his audience. . . . [In October 1952], for example, twenty-five radio stations faced possible disciplining by the Federal Communications Commission as a consequence of trying to stay out of trouble with their listeners. All of them chose not to antagonize their audiences by giving time for a speech by a candidate they regarded as a Communist sympathizer.

The Federal Communications Act, though it states specifically that radio stations are under no compulsion to put any politician on the air, also makes the general observation that stations should be operated "in the public interest, convenience and necessity." Among politicians, not surprisingly, that phrase is interpreted to include the broadcast of politicians' campaign oratory. Members of the FCC, being political appointees, have given no indication of dissenting from that view.

The FCC insists that during campaigns stations should broadcast an "adequate" volume of rival political claims. How much time the FCC considers adequate has never been defined, though it once rebuked a chain of Texas radio stations that had merely offered a half-hour apiece (plus additional time depending upon the program commitments of the stations and the desires of the candidates) to each of fifty-six candidates for state office.

To abstain from political programming can cost a broadcaster his license, but to participate in it can cost him his shirt. The political broadcast section of the Communications Act prohibits stations from censoring so much as a single word from any can-

[3] From "The Broadcasters' Ordeal by Politics," by Edwin H. James, senior editor. *Broadcasting and Telecasting. Fortune.* 46:105+. November 1952. Reprinted by special permission of the editors. Copyright 1952 by Time Inc.

didate's speech, even if the speech contains defamatory statements for which the station can be sued.

. . . [In 1951] the FCC placed WDSU, of New Orleans, on a "temporary" license, a condition not unlike that of the defendant in a murder trial while the jury is out. WDSU's offense was that it had refused to put on the air a mayoralty candidate whose speech the station considered libelous. The FCC eventually restored WDSU's license but it served firm notice that if any station from then on tampered with any candidate's speech, it might as well shut down.

Undoubtedly there have been cases in which stations deleted libel from political speeches without ever being hauled up before the FCC. Under promise of anonymity the manager of a radio station in a small southern town recently reported an awkward situation involving a candidate for sheriff who was unable to deliver his speeches from script because he was illiterate. "His ad libs were a caution," the manager said. "We solved that one by recording his stuff and editing it completely before broadcast." That action was, of course, a flagrant violation of the law, but it seemed a more practical course than letting the candidate go unedited. The station gambled that if the man could not read he would not be apt to write a complaint to the FCC.

There is no regulation preventing broadcasters from requesting advance scripts from politicians who are lettered enough to use them. Nor is there anything to prevent broadcasters from attempting to *persuade* speakers to eliminate objectionable passages. Most stations and networks do both. Usually speakers yield to reasonable argument. If they do not, however, the station must put them on the air, libel and all.

One Idaho case, six years old, still gives broadcasting executives the jitters. The manager of KIDO, Boise, after going over the transcription of a speech by Senator Glen Taylor, asked the Idaho Central Democratic Committee to kill some references to the Boise *Statesman* that he considered libelous. The committee refused and threatened to complain to the FCC if the speech were not broadcast intact.

KIDO put the speech on the air, and the *Statesman* promptly sued for $100,000 damages. Four other Idaho stations, booked by the Democrats for rebroadcast of the same speech, were then confronted with the morose choice of broadcasting the speech and defending the inevitable libel suits or rejecting it and risking FCC action. Suits would only cost money, while FCC reprisal could put them out of business. The stations carried the speech; each was sued for $100,000. The cases never went to trial, but it took three years and $10,000 to settle them.

The costs of defending and settling a more recent libel action against four Philadelphia stations were appreciably higher. The suit was filed in Federal district court against WCAU, WFIL, WPEN, and KYW by a man who complained he was defamed in a speech by the chairman of the Republican Central Committee of Philadelphia. The District Court returned a verdict for the defendants on the grounds that Section 315 of the Communications Act prohibited the stations from censoring the speech and therefore made them immune to libel actions. If this verdict had withstood appeal, broadcasters would have slept better ever since. The same old insomnia persists, however, for the . . . Court of Appeals reversed the judgment and the . . . Supreme Court, to which KYW took the case, refused to review it. . . . The stations negotiated a settlement with the plaintiff to avoid further expense. Each paid him $1,000. The legal costs were, of course, much greater.

Libel is only one problem vexing broadcasters when political campaigns are on. Another is the handling of requests for time from candidates of splinter parties.

In those states where they are on the ballot, the candidates of the Greenback, Prohibition, Socialist, Socialist Workers, or Vegetarian party are entitled to the same time (on the same terms) that is given or sold to the Republicans or Democrats. So are the Progressive party candidates. And so are the Communists, if they happen to be running their own candidates rather than supporting the Progressives.

In these days no network or station will endear itself to large numbers of listeners or viewers by lending its facilities to an acknowledged Communist or the candidate of a Communist front. But the courts and the FCC have seen to it that broadcasters have no choice.

Following the [1952] conventions of the Republican and Democratic parties, the Progressive party sent a letter to 439 radio stations and ninety-four television stations that had broadcast the acceptance speeches of Eisenhower and Nixon, and Stevenson and Sparkman. The Progressives demanded that the stations give equal time for acceptance speeches of the Progressive candidates, Vincent Hallinan for President and Mrs. Charlotta Bass for Vice President.

The request was not without intricacies. The acceptance speeches for which the party demanded time had already been given at the Progressive convention, which preceded both the major-party conventions, and had been broadcast at the time by quite a few radio and television stations. The acceptance speech of Mr. Hallinan, however, had been delivered by his wife. Hallinan was unable to speak for himself because of the meager broadcasting facilities at McNeil Island Federal prison, where he was serving a sentence for contempt of court.

Of the 533 radio and television stations to which the Progressive letter was sent, twenty-five refused to comply. In early September the party asked the FCC to take action against them. As of mid-October the commission had not . . . acted, but the twenty-five stations, in sticking to their principles, would seem to have stuck out their necks. Technically, they may not have violated the law in refusing equal time to Hallinan, since he did not deliver his acceptance speech himself. But Mrs. Bass did deliver her acceptance speech.

The proportion of stations rejecting the Progressive demand to those yielding to it was fairly typical of station behavior. Broadcasters have not invariably acted with conspicuous courage in resisting unreasonable political demands. In defense of their timidity, however, it may be noted that licenses expire regularly (every three years for radio stations, annually for television stations) and must be renewed on a showing that the stations have fully lived up to the law and FCC regulations. Further, not many stations can easily afford the costs of the litigation that can be anticipated if they buck up against strong political pressures or the FCC. . . .

Any real relief from the political broadcasting dilemma must come from an improvement in the basic law governing broadcasting. Three amendments to Section 315, all intended to correct inequities, were introduced in Congress . . . [in 1952] as part of a general overhauling given the Communications Act. None of the three was passed, however, and the only change made in Section 315 was a new restriction on the broadcasters' discretion. Congress, with an eye on the approaching campaigns, outlawed the fairly general practice of charging premium rates for political broadcasts. Some stations had been charging extra rates to discourage excessive political broadcasting, others to compensate for the special hazards involved, including poor credit risks. Some had in mind the net losses sometimes incurred when a political talk preempts time regularly occupied by a commercial sponsor, who must be rebated not only for the time charges but also for talent costs, if his talent commitments extend over a contract period. Quite a few stations charged premium political rates simply because that has been common practice among newspapers, which of course are not regulated by the government.

Some congressional leaders have indicated a willingness to consider legislation that would reduce the libel dangers confronting broadcasters. One recent proposal . . . is that the United States Criminal Code be amended to make it a crime for anyone to utter defamatory statements on the air. If a candidate insisted he was going ahead with the broadcast of a speech the station considered libelous, the broadcaster could appeal to the Federal district attorney or even go to court to enjoin the commission of a crime.

Such a safety measure would give the broadcaster some of the discretionary powers that the proprietors of other communications media can exercise over political material. He cannot hope, of course, to achieve the same freedom of decision the press enjoys. It is not his but the public's air that he uses.

Broadcasters are not asking for authority to censor ideology out of political oratory. And thoughtful men in the industry realize that the distinction between libel and "hard-hitting" campaigning is not always an easy one to make. They would like to feel some confidence, however, that they will not be driven out of business or into court every time an election approaches.

PRIVATE SPONSORSHIP AND PUBLIC
INDIFFERENCE [4]

The . . . [fact] that broadcasts of . . . [the 1952] nominating
conventions and the whole presidential campaign . . . [were]
"sponsored" on at least three of the television networks . . .
[was] greeted with an indifference far more significant than the
fact itself. . . .

So far as I know, the subject of commercial sponsorship for
the prime political activity of the American citizen has not been
prominently discussed on the air; no town meetings have been
held; no congressional comment has been reported. A few newspapers muttered disconsolately about commercialism, but this
was ascribed to pure jealousy of their rivals. Beyond that—
nothing. There are diseases of the mind in which apathy is a
morbid symptom; apparently one of them has attacked the national mind.

I shall return to this phenomenon after canvassing the questions which should have been asked.

First, since campaign coverage . . . [brought] the networks
. . . [millions of] dollars, was it necessary to break the tradition
of giving free time for political discussion *before* the nominating conventions? . . . The withdrawal of free time is in spirit
a violation of the principle of open discussion, a brutal declaration that the man with the most money behind him can have
most frequent access to the public, the man with no money can
have none. After the nominations, each candidate is backed by
party funds, and the propriety of selling time for campaigning
is allowed; before the conventions, in the past, leading candidates
have received free opportunity to appear, and this in turn has
meant free opportunity for the public to judge.

The FCC rules for broadcasters do not compel the gift of
time; they insist only that if time is given, it must be equally
divided between the parties. The new policy makes the rules
look silly: *who's giving time?* In a grim way, though, the prin-

[4] From "Politics—Televised and Sponsored," by Gilbert Seldes, writer on and
critic of the arts. *Saturday Review*. 35:30-1. March 15, 1952. Reprinted by
permission.

ciple of equality is upheld—a great tradition is dead, and in death we are all equal.

The second question is formalistic. How . . . [did] the sponsors (Admiral, Westinghouse, and Philco) figure in the proceedings? There are three possibilities. One is straight sponsorship: Westinghouse (fanfare) gives you the Republican National Convention; Admiral (cheers) presents (late on election night) the next President of the United States; Philco (massed bands) brings you (on inauguration day) the President of the United States. . . .

The intermediate manner which . . . [was] used, is for the sponsor to present "as a public service," the conventions, etc. This phrase, which used to mean specifically a program brought to the public by the broadcasting system or station at cost to itself without reimbursement from a sponsor, has now become a dodge which shifts uneasily between equivocation and hypocrisy.

The third, the thoroughly acceptable method, is for the networks to comply with the terms of their licenses and present the campaigns in the public interest with commercial messages at appropriate intervals. . . . Sponsorship associates a product with the content of a broadcast; commercial spots do nothing of the sort; in the first, the sponsor is, as his name implies, responsible; in the second, the network is.

My next question was answered in advance in the manner of "Needless to say the sponsor will have no control over the broadcasts, which will be handled by the network staffs." It is, of course, "unthinkable" that a sponsor should prejudice the report of a political event, but I have found that the "unthinkable" is often what a lot of people are thinking. The position of the networks would be stronger if the meager precedents we have were entirely satisfactory. . . . [In 1948] John Crosby reported a bit of showmanship out of the Philadelphia convention which was just this side of faking. When the Southern Democrats left the hall, the NBC-*Life* combination . . . showed them tearing their badges from their lapels and throwing them away. It was a dramatic symbol of their feelings, but it was not a spontaneous action—they had been asked to do it by the director of the broadcast. When it was over, the delegates scrabbled through the pile and pinned their own badges on again. . . .

Life magazine figures in the next question also. Its planned sponsorship of the [1952] Dumont telecasts . . . fell through because not enough stations were available; one reason they were not, *Variety* says, was that some stations, including the one owned by the Chicago *Tribune*, didn't want broadcasts sponsored by a magazine which has declared for Eisenhower. This seems a victory for nonsponsorship, but it leaves an uneasy feeling. *Life*'s politics were publicly made known; is it possible that the other sponsors have no political preferences?

I put two further questions without comment: What would happen to the coverage of the campaign if only one network got a sponsor and the others didn't? Would the audience of the nonsponsored stations get an adequate report? And what would happen if we had three parties, . . . the third being no more and no less radical than that of Henry Wallace; would sponsors be willing to associate themselves with an unpopular movement or would this be covered "as a public service"?

And for the future, I am curious to know whether, in 1956, the party managers won't ask to be paid for the show they are putting on, each delegate becoming a member of AFRA, and the party coffers swelling agreeably.

I submit these as matters of concern to the American people and submit also my own answer (none too good) to the riddle of the apparent indifference of the public. I think the questions haven't been asked because no medium, no channel, no habit of asking questions exists. . . . The magnitude of the problems raised by television is frightening; those relating to education, to children, to crime, to public inquiries are as important as the issues I have been discussing. Considering this, isn't it vitally important to create local groups to watch what television does and to give the public a medium for airing its doubts and dissents? . . .

A group of citizens in every community, drawn from lunch clubs and labor unions and professional groups and parent-teacher associations and religious bodies and all other important organizations, would actually give us a cross-section of the entire audience. Since the broadcasters want this audience and insist they give it only what it demands, they cannot object to observation and criticism and constructive suggestions—they might even win a deal of praise.

Such local groups could be loosely organized into regional sections leading to a national body which would be relatively small. Although I am not sanguine, I repeat a suggestion I have made before: that the broadcasters look benignly on the formation of these groups and, when they make their annual report on the state of television, give time for the discussion of the report on television itself.

I may be wrong in thinking that people would observe, comment, question, and, when necessary, protest if a channel for these activities were available. If I am wrong, it means that apathy has gone far enough to kill our natural reaction to political stimuli. It means that our responses are deadened and we have become social robots, taking whatever is brought to us, always grateful, answering the phone to say what program we are listening to, buying the products we are told to buy—and never thinking for ourselves. If that is so, it is a broadcaster's paradise, and the broadcasters themselves have done a lot to create it in the sweet land that once was the home of independent, thinking American citizens who were not afraid to ask questions.

LAW-MAKING ON TELEVISION [5]

Despite great reluctance on the part of many members and spirited opposition from a few, radio station WKY-TV, Oklahoma City, undertook this year one of the greatest public services that could be rendered by a communications medium for the benefit of good government. It began the televising of the [Oklahoma] Legislature in action. Many feel that it is the closest approach to a revival of the old New England town meeting type of government that is possible in these days of "big government."

[5] From "Televising the Legislature in Oklahoma," by Paul Harkey, Member, Oklahoma House of Representatives. *State Government*. 24:249-50+. October 1951. Reprinted by permission.

From the standpoint of the legislators WKY-TV almost
slipped in on them to begin the series of broadcasts. When
P. A. Sugg, manager of the station, first suggested that he would
be willing to cancel two paid programs each week in order to
televise the legislature, his proposal was not greeted too enthusi-
astically either by the legislature or the press of Oklahoma. One
House member called it "the silliest thing I've ever heard of"
and went on to explain: "One man can get up and make a fool
of himself, and the people back home would think we were all
that way." . . .

After a thorough discussion the House Committee on Rules
and Procedure gave the go-ahead signal on televising the opening session of Oklahoma's 23rd Legislature, and the Governor's
address a week later. Prior to each session, Edna Gibson, the
Executive Secretary of the State Cosmetology Board set up a
make-up bar ouside the House Chamber, where each legislator
could get properly made up for the television broadcast. There
were no takers for the offered embellishment, but the number
who approached and shied away indicates that it may have been
fear of ridicule that kept some of the legislators from making
themselves more "telegenic."

After the first two telecasts, most of the opposition in the
legislature faded, and the individual members realized that TV
was here to stay as long as WKY-TV desired to avail itself of
the opportunity.

Probably the strongest reaction for the televised sessions set
in when people on the street would comment to individual legislators that what they saw on television was so different from what
"political" newspaper reports had represented a situation to be.
Individual legislators began to realize that in television their
true actions were being presented without editing or bias, and
that television could be depended upon accurately to show the
people of Oklahoma what their legislature was doing.

The immediate results included improvement in decorum—
not that the Oklahoma Legislature had any lack of it, but the
customary reading of newspapers while in session, feet on desks,
small caucuses held in the aisles, etc., were nonexistent while the
camera's red light was on. Some members would groom themselves more carefully on days when they were to be televised;

the grooming sometimes took the form of adding certain individual characteristics by which a member could be identified more speedily on the floor. . . .

During the telecast, two cameras mounted one in each gallery are constantly in use. The director, stationed outside in the mobile transmitter, picks the best presentation from his monitoring screen, and if he wants a close-up shot of a single individual, or a "middle distance" shot of a group, he instructs the cameraman. . . .

Ewing Canaday, one of Oklahoma's outstanding radio reporters, did all the comment and narrative of the telecasts. His performance was superb in that he only laid down for his listeners the basic scene and avoided interrupting the continuity unless the lawmakers got into a complicated parliamentary tangle, where comment was necessary. These situations arise rather frequently, when the entire play changes hands—for example when a motion to table has been made—and without able comment the television audience could become confused. The Speaker had the Chief Clerk of the House of Representatives sit with Mr. Canaday during all telecasts of the House, so that together they could untangle for the people a procedural situation that the House had difficulty in untangling for itself.

There must be a thorough understanding with the program director and cameramen concerning just what actions of the legislators they will focus on, and what they will ignore. The question of libel or slander (whichever it might be in the event of televised defamation) is present in that through confusion a member might be discredited. This could happen when someone seated without permission at the desk of a member was guilty of unlegislative conduct, and the camera would pick up in the same scene the name plate of the member at whose desk the scene occurred. Such minor infractions as reading newspapers, important private conversations between members, etc., should be avoided by the cameras. Rules cannot be devised that will cover all situations of this type, but, with sympathetic cooperation between program director, cameramen, Speaker, and floor leader, situations will be avoided which might unfairly reflect discredit on an individual member, or which might make the radio station liable. . . .

It is the consensus of Oklahoma's legislators that television of the legislature is here to stay. Few of the disadvantages predicted for it materialized, and it took only one or two TV-fan letters to make an opponent say it was not too much of a nuisance.

In addition to the fan mail and telephone calls received, WKY-TV received responses which were most gratifying to its management. The general comment of those was that the people of Oklahoma appreciated the public service that was being rendered them by WKY-TV, and were not only enjoying the legislative telecasts, but were taking a new interest in state government.

Needless to say, legislators sometimes receive criticism as well as commendation from citizens. Sometimes, moreover, the reaction from individuals of the television audience may reflect insufficient grasp of issues involved. There are dangers, of course—for example, the danger that oversimplified public impressions may result from televising only one part of a given debate, or that dramatic skill may outweigh other qualities in impressing some of the audience. But most new technical developments involve some perils and are subject to abuse.

Television unquestionably brings lawmakers and the public into closer contact. It increases the ability of the people to form their own judgments of legislative actions, not depending wholly on second-hand accounts or some other individual's interpretation. Sound programming, with care by the legislature itself to bring truly representative examples of transaction of important public business to the public, can minimize any dangers. In Oklahoma most of us are convinced that solid values fully justify legislative television—that it is a genuine tool of democracy, for keeping government close to the people.

SHOULD CONGRESS BE TELEVISED? [6]

"I have the feeling," Senator Estes Kefauver told a Senate subcommittee many months ago, "that our government 'of the

[6] From an article by Robert Bendiner, writer on political affairs. *Collier's.* 131:62-5. January 17, 1953. Reprinted by permission.

people' and 'for the people' should become more and more a government 'by the people.' " And how better to achieve that end, he suggested, than by bringing the processes of government into their living rooms through the cool, impartial eye of television?

If the Senator and like-minded colleagues have their way, our national legislators will soon be as familiar to the public as Arthur Godfrey, Milton Berle or Tom Corbett, Space Cadet. But before they have their way they will know they have been in a battle.

Their lofty plans to televise the doings of Congress have evoked an equally lofty opposition. What looked to its proponents like an indisputable advance in the art of government has touched off a warm debate in Washington that cuts across party lines as few issues have done.

At first glance, nothing could seem fairer or simpler than the proposition that the business of Congress is most intimately the business of the people, and that therefore an effective instrument of direct communications should be used to lay that business before them. The two visitors' galleries in Congress testify to the acknowledged right of citizens to observe their representatives in action, but that right is limited by the fact that the House gallery accommodates just 616 persons, the Senate 621. Television would introduce no new principle; it would merely push back the walls of those chambers from Capitol Hill to Seattle and add seats—twenty, thirty, forty million of them.

Would these seats ever be used? Leaders in the movement to televise Congress, spearheaded by New York's Republican Representative Jacob K. Javits, cite the enthusiastic response to telecasts of United Nations sessions, the popular radio broadcasts of the Australian and New Zealand parliaments, the successful appearance of the Oklahoma state legislature on TV,[7] and the telecasts of the Senate Crime Committee hearings in 1951.

At their peak, the hearings of Kefauver's committee held audiences of from ten to twenty million Americans. Dust gathered on floor and furniture, meals went uncooked and marketing undone as housewives sent the normal Hooper rating of

[7] See selection above, "Law-Making on Television."—Ed.

1.5 per cent for a weekday winter morning in New York City
to a high of 34.5. Office work, too, suffered where TV sets were
available, and a spokesman for the movie industry complained
that the telecasts were worse for business "than a double-header
World Series."

The appeal of the Kefauver "show," running hour after hour
and day after day, was fairly described by the New York *Times*
as a "major phenomenon of our time." Its interest apparently
carried over to other aspects of government. A Gallup poll
found that 70 per cent of the voting population considered the
televising of Congressional sessions "a good idea" and 78 per
cent believed such programs would "be interesting." The ground-
work for such a project seemed to be well laid, the objective was
acknowledged to be worthy and the facilities were available.
Could critics seriously object?

They could and they did. Indeed, after the Kefauver hearings the cause of televising government suffered sharp reverses.
Even while the crime committee telecasts were in progress, the
Federal Bar Association of New York, New Jersey and Connecticut warned against their "glaring melodrama." Other top legal
groups were equally critical, and the American Bar Association
ultimately condemned all radio and television coverage of Congressional investigating committee hearings. [In March 1952]
New York's legislature, with Governor Dewey's endorsement,
banned the televising, broadcasting or filming of any official state
proceeding to which witnesses may be subpoenaed.

On the national front, the cause fared as badly. In February
1952, Sam Rayburn, then Speaker of the House, banished the
television camera, along with radio broadcasts, recordings and
films, from committee hearing rooms. Rayburn singled out TV
in his edict, advising all chairmen that "there is no rule of the
House permitting televising of House proceedings." On the
other side of the Capitol, Senator Pat McCarran of Nevada sponsored a resolution that would have banned news photographers
as well as movie and TV cameras. Several senators greeted the
proposal to televise sessions with such unparliamentary adjec-
tives as "silly" and "crackpot."

And, as though to make a clean sweep for the opposition, . . . [in October 1952] United States District Judge Henry A. Schweinhaut acquitted two Cleveland gamblers of contempt of Congress, ruling that they were justified in refusing to testify before the Kefauver committee under distracting conditions caused, at least in part, by TV cameras.

Why all this opposition? What are the arguments against television on Capitol Hill—and are they irrefutable?

No doubt the most complicated of all the problems involved is the difficulty of selecting, without political bias, what should and what should not go out over the air waves. Besides the two chambers themselves, there are usually more than 40 standing, special and select committees, many of them spawning two or three subcommittees, all entitled to hold hearings at their pleasure. If all presently available channels were placed exclusively at the disposal of Congress, they would be unable to carry the total volume of activity (nor could the public possibly absorb it).

No one envisions more than a fraction of such coverage, of course, and that's where the difficulty comes in. Someone would have to decide, on any given day, what part of the activity of Congress was best for the American people to witness. It would be for him to say, for example, whether they should see and hear a House subcommittee thrash out a new tax bill, the Senate Foreign Relations Committee grill experts on our Far Eastern policy, or the House as a whole debate amendments to the Taft-Hartley Act. Clearly, this power would be far-reaching, and it would grow as people came to depend more and more on their television sets for an understanding of political issues.

The danger, as opponents of Congressional TV see it, is that politics would dictate the choices. Would a Democratic Speaker of the House, if he were the one to decide, be likely to give TV time to a committee bent on exposing alleged corruption by Democrats? No more than a Republican Speaker would single out a debate likely to cost the GOP votes at the next election. Furthermore, what would prevent this all-powerful program director from, let us say, telecasting the upper house on Monday, when Senator Dingbat has arranged to deliver a powerful speech for boosting the olive-oil tariff, and turning the cameras elsewhere on Tuesday, when Senator Wingding rises to tear the olive-oil lobby to shreds?

The Senate's present rules of debate are, in fact, made to order for just this kind of discrimination. Since a member may rise at almost any time and discuss anything for as long as he wants, coherent debate such as television enthusiasts foresee would be purely a matter of luck. Discussing the subject with Javits over TV, Republican Senator Wallace F. Bennett of Utah put the case bluntly:

"The way the Senate operates, it is impossible to set up a debate as a series of speeches that follow each other. A Senator would say what he wanted to say on the subject, and then his colleagues would have a week or two to think over what he said and decide just what their reaction was. I'm sure you realize that if you would attempt to set up the Senate so that you could televise a . . . great debate you would have to completely destroy . . . the tradition and rules of the Senate."

With this same power of choice extended to committee hearings, what would prevent the viewers' getting only partial, one-sided testimony? Or what would keep a committee chairman from scheduling certain witnesses at nine in the morning, when few citizens are watching, and others at eight in the evening, when a telecast would have the eyes and ears of the country? Those who favor televising hearings usually insist that coverage be complete, so the public can get a fair picture, but to follow the doings of a single committee for months would be to curtail drastically the televising of other congressional activity of possibly greater importance.

If, on the other hand, there is to be selectivity, Heaven help the selector. He would be so barraged by lobbyists and special pleaders, he would be under such pressures of party and of conscience, that his position would soon be unendurable. Yet if the choices were left to majority vote, the party in control could stack the air waves to its perpetual advantage. The problem of how to choose what should be televised is formidably complex, and involves principle as well as procedure. . . .

Outsiders who suggest that TV would bring out the ham in our representatives might be accused of indulging in the time-honored American game of baiting Congress. But many members of that body do more than suggest it. Discussing the question on a TV show, Representative Richard Bolling, a Missouri Democrat, remarked, "It is human nature to put on a show if you have a big audience," and added, "a lot of people can be very easily fooled by a smooth actor or a slick demagogue." Republican Senator Alexander Wiley of Wisconsin warns of the danger that "a yearning for the TV limelight could cause a turning from the facts by legislators, could cause an outbreak of hammy theatrics, rather than continuous serious debate."

A number of senators have offered the opinion that the upper house would never get any work done if television cameras were on hand to put a premium on rhetoric. The point draws further strength from the comment of several United Nations officials to the effect that television and radio have made diplomacy difficult in that organization. Each session, in the words of one delegate, "turns into a propaganda battle . . . using . . . the United Nations as a platform for political and psychological warfare, rather than for negotiations."

People who feel that congressional immunity is sometimes abused add still another count to the indictment. If a citizen may be damaged now by a false denunciation on the floor of Congress or by a committee witness, it is a cinch, they say, that he will be far more seriously hurt if assaulted with the aid of television— especially since he enjoys no comparable facilities for rebuttal. Such procedure, Senator Wiley warns, "can lay the basis for slander to a degree which we have heretofore never con- ceived." . . .

Beyond these questions lies what some members consider the worst stumbling block of all. Who would foot the enormous bill for bringing Congress to your TV screen? As a major figure in the controversy, Congressman Javits sounded out the leading networks on the subject. In general, they reflected a keen interest in covering both hearings and Congressional sessions, and indi- cated a willingness to absorb the costs—if they had the power to select. Coverage, said the National Broadcasting Company, "should be on the basis of news merit," with television accorded "the same access to important news events as the press services, newsreels and newspapers have."

Even for this limited coverage, it is doubtful, as Republican Senator Styles Bridges of New Hampshire has pointed out, that the networks could afford indefinitely to do the job as a public service. The other possibilities are commercial sponsorship, government sponsorship, and the establishment of a government-owned network. All three present formidable problems.

Many congressmen feel that it would be undignified, not to say dangerous, for a government to have its official activities selected and brought to the television audience as a commercial venture. There is a legal aspect to the question, too. As experienced a lawyer as Morris Ernst feels that witnesses compelled by subpoena to perform, as it were, for a private sponsor's benefit may well be justified in bringing suit—especially in the case of those who, like teetotalers and vegetarians, may find themselves helping sell products to which they object on principle.

Yet economy-minded congressmen take a chilly view of adding TV costs to the national budget. And they think even less of setting up a government-owned network, a notion that to some legislators, as [Republican] Senator Karl Mundt of South Dakota has indicated, smacks of socialism.

The difficulty of using the TV camera fairly, possible injustice to witnesses, encouraging of demagogues, and the tricky question of financing—these, then, are the substance of the case against televising Congress. It is an impressive case, and advocates of the proposal do not minimize it, but they are confident that in the end they will win. Basically, their confidence rests on the belief that people want to see their Congress in action, that for the sake of good government they should see it, that it is mechanically possible for them to do so—and that any difficulties in the way should and will be eliminated. . . .

[As for] the thorny question of financing, the forces of TV admit that they have no final answer. They are for starting slowly and feeling their way as they go. Javits is willing to give the commercial networks a chance to operate as a public service. If this coverage doesn't prove adequate, "government-operated facilities might be set up to do the job."

The Senate Crime Investigating Committee approved private sponsorship, but it proposed certain checks. A committee would have the right, for example, to pass upon the sponsor secured by the network, keeping in mind the dignity of the business at hand. No commercial announcements would be permitted from the hearing room or while testimony was in progress. Only austere and dignified announcements would be allowed, such as, "These hearings are brought to you as a public service by the X Company in cooperation with the Y Television Network."

Some members of Congress, frankly uncertain, want a commission to be appointed to make a thorough study of the whole question of facilities, costs and sponsorship.

Other suggestions range all the way to the demand of the United Automobile Workers' union for federally owned and operated networks that would cover much of the Congressional scene, coming as close as possible to providing the "air equivalent of the *Congressional Record*."

The Javits bill . . . does not call for anything like continuous coverage of House sessions. Like nearly all other sponsors of the plan, the New York congressman opposes the televising of routine sessions as neither practical nor of value. What he wants to see beamed to the voters are the "really critical and vital" debates, and these, he thinks, can be scheduled and tightened up to a greater degree than many senators and representatives are willing to concede.

In the House, the decision on what to televise would rest with the Speaker, who presumably would follow the sense of the chamber as a whole. On the other side of the Capitol, the burden would fall similarly on the presiding officer, or the Senate itself would vote its pleasure. The regular give-and-take of congressional practice and the possibility of future retaliation for gross partiality are counted on to assure fair play.

Major debates, Javits suggests, might be held at night, with time equally divided between the parties and limits fixed for each speaker. Would this fly in the face of Senate rules? "Then it is in the public interest that the Senate rules shall be changed." It is at this point that old hands on Capitol Hill look for rough weather, for the Senate will not easily be pried loose from its vulnerable and cherished tradition of unlimited debate.

Javits, Kefauver, Wiley and many other members of Congress are acutely aware of the danger that witnesses may be victimized by the television camera, but they feel this need not be the case. Technicians can, and have, minimized the glare, noise and heat. Actually, many public figures find TV less distracting than news-reel apparatus and the flashing of the press photographer's bulbs. Kefauver has proposed fixing up a large caucus room for televised hearings, with glass compartments such as the United Nations provides for TV crews and equipment.

On the more complex question of giving witnesses fair treatment, the TV forces are quick to point out that if procedures are unjust, they should be corrected whether or not the camera is trained on them. To this end, several members are pressing for the adoption of a fair code to be followed by all congressional investigating committeees. Kefauver would give all persons whose reputations have been jeopardized an opportunity for immediate rebuttal and he would also allow a limited cross-examination of witnesses, among other guarantees.

The argument that television would aggravate the injustice of unfair attack on private citizens from the floor of Congress is a bit harder to overcome. Members would, of course, continue to enjoy their constitutional immunity from libel action. But Javits would allow the injured citizen to sue the government, thus giving him a chance for possible vindication in a court of law and at the same time discouraging recklessness on Capitol Hill. He makes the further point that should a congressman get careless in his charges, quick refutation by his colleagues would be more effective on television than in the press, where only those readers who go beyond the headlines and the first paragraph would ever encounter it.

As for the hamming that some predict, TV advocates think there would be less of it before the camera than there is now. There is now more incentive for such sensationalism, they say, since in large sections of the country Congress gets scant attention in the press and it takes something of a stunt to put a lawmaker on the front page. Besides, they say, the more demagogues expose themselves to public observation, the less the public will stand for them. . . .

On this score, as on others, the pro-television forces point to experience. An authoritative observer of the effects of radio broadcasts from New Zealand's House of Representatives is quoted to show that citizens of that country have responded "very quickly and very critically to conduct which does not conform to accepted ideas of parliament as a dignified and very serious institution." A rather critical commentator on Australia's similar experiment concedes that in spite of some disagreement as to whether the tone of debate has been improved, "some members . . . might still be in parliament if the microphone had not so mercilessly exposed their shortcomings." . . .

What heartens TV's champions on Capitol Hill is that the arguments of their opponents in Washington are the same arguments that were once heard in Canberra, Wellington and Oklahoma City. Yet regular radio broadcasts of their national legislatures have become a popular fixture in the lives of Australians and New Zealanders, easily surviving changes of government in both countries.

CAN TV SERVE JUSTICE? [8]

One evening early . . . [in 1951] I arrived home after working rather late at the office. Instead of finding my family finishing dinner as I had expected, I found them gathered around the television set. They were listening avidly to the proceedings of the Kefauver committee and I must admit that I promptly joined them. We all had a very belated dinner!

Few of us will soon forget the taut drama of the Kefauver hearings. They set many Americans to pondering anew on the role of television in modern affairs. . . . The public generally liked the televising of the Kefauver commmittee hearings. This stems in part from the traditional desire and right of the American people to know what their government is doing. Morbid

[8] From "Justice and TV," by William T. Gossett, General Counsel, Ford Motor Company. *American Bar Association Journal.* 38:15-18+. January 1952. Reprinted by permission.

curiosity and sensationalism undoubtedly also made a large contribution to the success of this startling innovation. But whatever the reason, there is little doubt that the widespread public acceptance of the telecasts has provided a powerful impetus to demands for television coverage of all sorts of official business. Indeed, it has been suggested that television might properly be extended into our courtrooms.

Consider, for example, the recent statement of Margaret Webster, noted theatrical producer. As quoted in the New York *Times,* Miss Webster said she thought that televising, if it could be done without disturbing courtroom procedures, would be beneficial.

"I believe", she said, "that the American public, when it is directly confronted with it, has the capacity for recognizing the 'ring of truth.' "

Miss Webster appears to assume an inherent right on the part of the public to try a case in their living rooms.

Although most lawyers have condemned the suggestion (and many bar associations already are on record in this respect), some have supported it. Rudolph Halley, who as counsel for the Kefauver committee became well-known almost overnight, is one of these. He not only supports the televising of the committee's activities but argues that, since the press coverage of some criminal trials is of such a nature that "the circus is on," the best way to get the full scene before the public is to let in the video cameras.

I respect Mr. Halley's views, but here he seems to be saying that as long as a criminal trial is going to have a hippodrome quality anyway, there should be no objection to enlarging the tent. As valuable as human curiosity has been in the progress of mankind, I think its scope must nevertheless be limited where judicial issues are concerned. . . .

The primary purpose of congressional investigating committees is to seek out facts that will lead to the framing of wise legislation. Courts, on the other hand, are not concerned with the initiation of legislation; they are charged with applying the law and administering justice. Their concern is that, as between private parties, their respective rights are equitably adjusted, and in criminal cases, that justice is done as between the state and the accused.

Traditionally, our trials are held in public, and we are all so familiar with the concept of public trials that perhaps no one would question the right of an accused to have the public present at his trial. This is established by the Bill of Rights and is set forth as well in the laws of the various states. . . .

Until television came along . . . we generally recognized the right of the individual to have the protection of the public presence while at the same time not being made the object of idle curiosity and public scorn. An accused man is presumed innocent until proved guilty and his right to privacy has always been considered stronger than the right of the public to be entertained or even instructed. The inevitable injury to the defendant of being accused and tried far outweighs any public benefit which might ensue from enlarging the customary audience.

It is not unlikely that there will be trials which may appear to the public or the broadcasting companies to demand the presence of television cameras. Should the courts generally yield to such a demand, the possible injurious consequences to the administration of justice are manifold. Something other than justice could readily take hold of the imaginations of witnesses, lawyers, jurors and even judges should a television camera be introduced into a court of law.

The participants in the judicial process should have the single-minded purpose of arriving at justice. Justice is best administered in an atmosphere of objectivity and sober responsibility, and so courts traditionally have ruled out diversions, distractions and all things which might convert a trial into a carnival. For this reason even ordinary newspaper cameras are banned in many courtrooms.

Obviously, television is diversion and distraction on a grand scale. I am not satisfied with the argument that very shortly technological improvements will eliminate the need for special lighting and still the loud whir of the camera. These are the lesser distractions. The knowledge that an invisible audience of thousands or perhaps millions is viewing every move would be the greatest distraction. It should be manifest that the shattering prospect of having to testify and face searching cross-examination before a huge unseen audience is not calculated to produce reliable testimony from the witnesses—either for the state or the defense.

It has been suggested that an important beneficial effect derived from televising such stimulating events as major trials is that it would act as a deterrent to crime. But this is an ancient, discarded dogma which, I think, should not be revived. The same deterrent effect was sought when criminals were put in pillories in the public square, when witches were burned on windy hills, and when felons had their ears and noses cut off. . . .

I have discussed television in relation to courtroom proceedings because it seems to me that if the use of television is to be justified in connection with congressional investigations like those of the Kefauver committee, we would be well advised first to justify it with respect to proceedings in courts of law. This is so because, in court, the defendant is provided with all the safeguards that a carefully constructed system is able to provide: his right to be informed in advance of the nature of the charges against him; his right to be confronted with the witnesses against him and to subject them to cross-examination; his right to compulsory process for obtaining witnesses in his favor; his right to be represented by counsel; and his right to testify then and there in his own defense.

Let us now look at the proceedings of congressional investigative committees. Their investigations admittedly are not judicial in nature; their purpose is to explore but not to judge except as to whether legislation should be drawn. Historically, their functions have been, first, to seek information that will enable Congress to legislate wisely; and second, to determine whether executive and administrative agencies are properly performing their functions with respect to the enforcement of law or the expenditure of public funds.

Certainly no one would deny the power of Congress to investigate. Indeed, congressional investigations are among the most important of legislative functions. When, however, congressional investigations assume the aspect of an individual trial, without the traditional safeguards of regular court proceedings, then the question becomes one of how to preserve the constitutional rights of citizens without impairing the functions of Congress. The question is not the objectives of congressional committees. The question is one of method and scope.

Consider, for example, congressional investigations into such matters as the St. Lawrence Waterway or Economic Aid to Europe. These investigations, just as those of the Kefauver committee, require the attendance of informed witnesses, and the public interest is very much at stake. Holding such investigations in public can hardly be open to question, and I suppose that few would object to televising their proceedings. This is so because there is little likelihood that any witness would be called to testify because of the reprehensible character of his personal views or behavior. And there is little chance that in giving evidence any witness would impugn the good name of a third party.

It is when congressional investigations seek to inquire into questions of personal wrongdoing, as distinguished from the impersonal questions of broad public policy, that the fundamental rights of individuals seem most likely to be infringed and therefore need the greatest protection. . . .

As we all know, in the exercise of its function, the Kefauver committee, following the usual practice of congressional investigative committees, brought before it numerous persons not charged with specific crime but who were believed to be engaged in wrongful conduct. It was sought to elicit from them facts which would provide the basis for Federal legislation. But these facts were also such as might tend to incriminate them in state courts and render them subject to prosecution.

It has been urged, however, that television of congressional committee hearings would tend to improve their procedures, and that personal rights of witnesses are subordinate to the public interest. In support of these propositions, James Lawrence Fly, formerly Federal Communications Commissioner, has said:

Unfairness in the procedure of hearings is in the control of the hearing officers. Improvements in fairness and in decorum are long overdue. TV can hardly impede, and may even accelerate, the move toward fair treatment.

There is no "right to privacy" in a legal public hearing. This is the public's business, and both the committee and the subjects are on public trial. . . .

It seems to me that the function of such congressional committees as the Kefauver committee resembles more the inquisitorial function of our grand juries than it does a trial.

We all know that the work of grand juries is undertaken in secret. One of the reasons for this is the need to protect the grand jury members from those whom they are investigating. Another is the need for concealing from the suspected citizen the fact that he is under investigation until he is formally charged. But these practical considerations are not the only reasons for grand jury secrecy. There is an even more important reason: In many cases, even if the persons involved were vindicated, they might be forever tarred by the mere fact that an inquisitorial body of the state had seen fit to scrutinize their conduct.

I do not suggest that congressional hearings be held in secret. But I do want to emphasize that, since in a grand jury proceeding a witness is not surrounded by the safeguards available to him in a trial, he is protected by the secrecy of the proceeding. In a congressional hearing, however, he has neither the safeguards of a trial nor the privacy of grand jury proceedings. Why, then, should the risk of irreparable damage to his reputation be compounded by introducing the television cameras?

Advocates of telecasting congressional hearings—even where the affairs of individuals are concerned—defend their position on the ground that television is merely another means of communication and as such should be treated no differently than the press. It should be pointed out, however, that neither Congress nor, as a general proposition, the courts have recognized the principle of equal access to all media of communication. The Senate and House have consistently barred radio, movies, and television from coverage of their sessions.

Recently, Dean Alfange, a prominent member of the New York Bar, summed up the matter succinctly when he said:

> Government business is not show business. It is the function of government to reconcile liberty with authority and freedom with organization. This is essentially a judicial process, even at the legislative level. It cannot operate at its best under the scrutiny of ubiquitous floodlights, before invisible galleries, and in the confusion of the clashing

elements of light and sound. The fulfillment of justice requires sober reflection and quiet deliberation. . . . If a hoodlum can be deprived of his rights today with public approbation, tomorrow an innocent man, by the same precedent, can also be deprived of his rights. . . . We must not permit any practice, however popular, to go unchallenged if it tends to weaken the fabric of the Bill of Rights.

It is apparent that the problem is susceptible of no simple, easy solution. Earnest and honest people holding all shades of opinion have joined in the debate. It is a modern restatement of the classic conflict of the rights of the individual against those of society, and of the rights of society against those of the individual.

I sincerely hope that the solution to the problem will be erected on the twin pillars of the orderly search for justice and the preservation of the essential rights of the individual.

For my own part, I should prefer that millions of people be denied the benefit of televised participation in congressional hearings than that the processes of justice be jeopardized or that the essential rights of the individual be denied.

BROADCASTING—GOOD, BAD, AND MEDIOCRE

EDITOR'S INTRODUCTION

The most frequently heard criticism of radio and television is that they are mediocre and imitative, where they could be outstanding and creative. The first three articles in this section spell out these charges.

Yet, as the usually sour professional critics are happy to admit, there are new ideas constantly stirring in broadcasting. Some of these new ideas take hold, but most of them die a-borning. The later articles in this section relate examples of such ideas. These, of course, are merely samples, and it should not be assumed that everyone agrees that even these ideas are wholly commendable or workable.

Like many other aspects of our American society, broadcasting is composed of a large middle ground generally accepted by the majority, and a few shining peaks. These "peaks" include pioneering achievements by broadcasting networks and stations themselves, as well as the participation of privately endowed foundations, local government, and organized listeners in the direction of broadcasting activities. But these stimuli to radio and television will have a real effect only if they win interest and support from the ordinary radio listener and television viewer.

TIME-TRAP FOR CHILDREN [1]

In a Boston suburb, a nine-year-old boy reluctantly showed his father a report card heavily decorated with red marks, then proposed one way of getting at the heart of the matter: they could give the teacher a box of poisoned chocolates for Christmas. "It's easy, Dad, they did it on television last week. A

[1] From "The Time-Trap," an editorial by Norman Cousins, Editor, *Saturday Review*. *Saturday Review of Literature*. 32:20. December 24, 1949. Reprinted by permission.

man wanted to kill his wife, so he gave her candy with poison in it and she didn't know who did it."

In Brooklyn, New York, a six-year-old son of a policeman asked his father for real bullets because his little sister "doesn't die for real when I shoot her like they do when Hopalong Cassidy kills 'em."

In Los Angeles, a housemaid caught a seven-year-old boy in the act of sprinkling ground glass into the family's lamb stew. There was no malice behind the act. It was purely experimental, having been inspired by curiosity to learn whether it would really work as well as it did on television.

The terror comic strips were bad enough, but they are rapidly on the way to playing squeaky second fiddles to television as prime movers in juvenile misconduct and delinquency. TV is hardly out of infancy as a major industry, but already it has become the nation's number one time-trap for children in those areas where video programs are available. And what makes terror on TV more effective than in comics is that it often enjoys the sanction of a family audience. When Johnnie and Mary sit down before the magic glass screen to take in an evening's entertainment, they often do so in the presence of Mother or Dad or both. This unspoken parental benediction hovers over the electronic eye as it tells the story of the inevitable love triangle which becomes a twosome via the equally inevitable device of the poisoned highball glass, or the story of a gang war in which corpses are strewn about like popcorn at a circus.

It would be easy but unfair, however, to load *all* the blame on the parents. Part, at least, must be reserved for television itself. Here, in concept at least, was the most magnificent of all forms of communication. Here was the supreme triumph of invention, the dream of the ages—something that could bring directly into the home a moving image fused with sound— reproducing action, language, and thought without loss of measurable time. Here was the magic eye that could bring the wonders of entertainment, information, and education into the living room. Here was a tool for the making of a more enlightened democracy than the world had ever seen.

Yet out of the wizardry of the television tube has come such an assault against the human mind, such a mobilized attack on the imagination, such an invasion against good taste as no other communications medium has known, not excepting the motion picture or radio itself. . . . Since television has been on an assembly-line basis, there has been mass-produced a series of plodding stereotypes and low-quality programs. Behind it all, apparently, is a grinding lack of imagination and originality which has resulted in the standardized television formula for an evening's entertainment: a poisoning, a variety show, a wrestling match.

To be sure, there are some chinks of light in the tunnel. But for every half hour worth seeing, there are literally days of wrath and writhing. For every first-rate entertainment program there are dozens of tank-town revues. For every Kukla, Fran, and Ollie program, which stimulates rather than stultifies the imagination of children, there are countless unskilled and ear-shattering kiddie shows and an even larger number of terror-and-torture specials. For every truly magnificent public-service feature such as the televising of the sessions of the United Nations or the NBC Symphony or the round-table forums . . . or the book-author programs, there are numberless time-fillers whose only function seems to be to keep the animated commercials from running together. For every top-notch sports event there are endless grunt-and-groan festivals that are supposed to pass for wrestling.

It is not as though television lacks men and women of stature on the planning end. . . . What has happened apparently is that the industry was honeycombed at the start with supposed crowd-pleasers who moved in on the ground-floor and promptly converted it into a sub-cellar. It was the same old story: the grotesque perpetuation of the fable about the intelligence of the average American—that it is somewhere on the level of the twelve-year-old child. This billion-dollar blunder has already come close to putting the skids under Hollywood, has devitalized and disfigured much of radio, and has wrecked some of the largest pulp magazines in America. Despite the evidence, TV is apparently using the same bubble for its foundation. What is needed is a prodigious raising of sights that takes into account the phenomenal rise in the national level of education, and, in general, the increasing maturity of the American people as measured by all available indices.

This is no argument for highbrowism or for the conversion of TV into an extension of the classroom. Television is essentially a medium of entertainment and enlightenment. But it is still light-years away in any truly vital and creative approach to the fabulous possibilities waiting to be recognized and realized.

In any event, all speculation over the future of television must begin with the hard truth that right now it is being murdered in the cradle.

"A CUT-RATE NICKELODEON" [2]

Let's face it: television is getting pretty bad. The high hopes for video which were held by so many are vanishing before our eyes. The medium is heading hell-bent for the rut of innocuity, mediocrity and sameness that made a drab if blatant jukebox of radio. The success of TV is proving a hollow and disheartening jest: television apparently can't stand prosperity.

Remember the proud words . . . of how television represented a vital new form of electronic theatre that augured an exciting and challenging new cultural era? Or how the imperishable wonders of a vibrant and articulate stage would be spread to the far corners of the land?

Look at the television giant! . . . Morning, noon and night the channels are cluttered with eye-wearying monstrosities called "films for television," half-hour aberrations that in story and acting would make an erstwhile Hollywood producer of "B" pictures shake his head in dismay. Is this the destiny of television: a cut-rate nickelodeon?

Or look what's happening in what may go down as the "I-Love-Lucy" era of television. Miss Lucille Ball and Desi Arnaz came up with a legitimate and true hit. Presto! The minions of TV take their cue. Let's all do situation comedy—absurd and

[2] From "The Low State of TV," by Jack Gould, Radio-Television Editor, New York Times. New York Times. p X 13. October 19, 1952. Reprinted by permission.

incredible little charades that would be hooted off the stage of the high school auditorium. Hold high the mask of make-believe? Put out the hambone!

Whither the drama? Where is the Tony Miner that proudly and unafraid gave TV a *Julius Caesar* to remember? What of the Celanese Theatre that had the dignity to scorn the censor's blue pencil? In their stead largely are elongated whodunits and soap operas that are embellished with production trickiness and glamour to obscure the vacuum that lies underneath.

What of the endless procession of crime thrillers that supinely worship at the throne of "action" as a substitute for characterization and suspense? And of the panel shows with the same faces appearing over and over again with monotonous regularity? They are ever with us.

And the children's programs? Is there no surcease from the nauseating trifles whereon the younger generation sing the praises of cereals and candy bars? Are these programs to be the sole measure of the child's inheritance of the riches of the library and the treasures of the arts? The death of television's Mr. I. Magination is a symbol, not a statistic.

Television must take heed. It is blindly and short-sightedly selling its ultimate greatness for a batch of synthetic popularity ratings that are boring into TV's foundations like termites. It is caught on the old radio treadmill of repetition and imitation in the wan and futile hope that it need not face up to the realities that lie ahead.

Sponsors and broadcasters fool only themselves—not their audiences nor their customers—if they think they can mold television into a pattern that is risk-proof and sure, as they are trying to do now. Their only security and their only insurance for the days ahead lies in bold recognition that, if television is to retain its vigor as an advertising form, they themselves must live excitingly.

Gentlemen, wake up! Out with artiness and the academic approach; let's talk business!

What's happening to television is a slow paralysis of its living organs. Now that the medium is fully accepted, the gentlemen who are paying the bills have decided to be content with the handful of program formulas that bring predictable results. They are being suckers for the bromidic contention that the American public can be divided up into several big chunks. Then just give 'em what they want, goes the cry.

Any industrialist who followed that line of archaic reasoning knows in his own heart he soon would be booted out of office by his board of directors or stockholders. How on earth did the public know it wanted cellophane? Or frozen orange juice? Or lifesaving penicillin at the price of a box of chocolates? They didn't have the foggiest concept of such things. It is the research, the imagination, and the willingness to take risks that made American industry what it is today and the source of uncountable blessings for a fuller and more enjoyable living.

This analogy holds true for television. To be content with the "products" of television as they stand now, merely because their acceptance by the public is beyond doubt, is to follow the most perilous course open to broadcasters and sponsors. It can only lead to one end: a constant shrinkage of the base upon which the whole medium rests.

If only in economic self-defense, the sponsors and broadcasters must now embark on a program of research and experimentation in television programming. This goal is not altruistic or intellectual; it is eminently practical. By constantly broadening and stimulating the public taste, the sponsors are widening the billboards upon which in future years they can paste their advertisements. If they are to use the arts for legitimate commercial ends, common sense dictates that they diversify those arts just as they diversify the output of their factories.

How is this to be done, asks the business man? Let's ask the business man a question: how does he meet such problems in his own business? Why does he have lawyers, engineers, chemists, foremen, personnel specialists?

In television the answer is the same. There are writers, actors, directors and producers who have devoted a lifetime to learning their specialized crafts. For heaven's sake let them do their jobs as they know they should be done.

Give the writers the chance to write what is in their hearts and consciences and give them the chance to say it in their own way. What do writers know of the problems of vice presidents in charge of sales; what do vice presidents in charge of sales know of the problems of writers?

Bring on the plays that have something to say and are not afraid to take a stand. Give the directors and producers the chance to try out those ideas that are departures from the norm. Encourage the exploration of ballet, opera, education, concerts, the lecture stage, religion, Restoration comedy, the classic. If the sponsor of every program on the air allowed a director to do just one experiment a year of his own choosing, think of what it would mean for the creative processes of television.

The leaders of broadcasting—those who own stations and those who directly influence its course by the programs they choose to sponsor—owe it not only to themselves but to the public as well to search their consciences.

Can they honestly maintain that our competitive free enterprise is so helpless, so unimaginative and so lacking in daring that the measure of success in television must be the popularity of mediocrity, not of excellence? They can give the answer only one way; on the screens of . . . [America's television] receivers.

SEVEN DEADLY SINS OF THE AIR [3]

Television, a young giant which does not yet know its own strength, has become a member of . . . [millions of] American homes. Eventually, despite delaying battles over color television, it will be in all of them, upsetting the household like any young obstreperous child. While it is still in its infancy, it might be well to lay down some rules about its table manners. If we value our sanity, we had better elevate television's deportment to a level much higher than that of its parent, radio.

Radio, of course, had many conspicuous virtues and seldom let us forget any of them. In 1926 it was the poor immigrant of the arts. By 1950 it had risen to fame and wealth, earned roughly $500 million a year and had built a shrine to broadcasting,

[3] From an article by John Crosby, radio-television critic of the New York *Herald Tribune*. *Life*. 29:147-8+. November 6, 1950. Reprinted by permission of the editors. Copyright 1950 by Time Inc.

Radio City, to which millions of Americans made pilgrimages every year to pay homage to Mary Margaret McBride. It penetrated into forty-two million American homes and brought Americans the renowned voices of incoming presidents, outgoing kings and Arthur Godfrey—to list them, more or less, in the reverse order of their importance. But radio, rich and powerful as it was, had some grave flaws in its character and, if the public and especially the broadcaster are not alerted in time, television will inherit all of them. Radio had a lot to answer for, which might be lumped under the heading of its Seven Deadly Sins.

1) Radio sold its soul to the advertiser

Broadcasting sold . . . [itself] to the advertiser before it was old enough to know what it was doing. Radio, of course, is not the only medium *supported* by advertising, but it is the only one owned outright by it. Newspapers and magazines take money from the advertiser too. Their product—some of it good, some of it awful—belongs to them and is controlled by them. In radio it is the other way around.

This situation is not entirely the fault of the broadcaster. Back in 1926, when radio first went commercial on a large scale, the advertiser came nosing around, trying to buy time as he would buy space on a billboard. But broadcasting then was largely in the hands of the engineers who were far more interested in producing a signal that could be heard clearly in Brooklyn than what that signal carried. These men had little experience or sympathy with show business. After a bit the advertiser got sick of hanging around waiting, and he went ahead and produced his own programs which radio stations were only too happy to broadcast in exchange for a certain amount of legal tender. So the advertiser—however reluctantly—got into show business up to his elbows. . . .

Well, the average advertising man is naturally attempting to sell the most goods to the most people. He feels—quite logically —that it is none of his business to fill a niche in broadcasting which everyone else is neglecting. In spite of a lot of clamor to the contrary, the advertiser doesn't give a hoot about putting on the air what the public wants to hear. . . . [In 1946] Paul

Lazarsfeld of Columbia University revealed in a national survey that 50 per cent of American women loathed soap opera. While gratifying the rather astonishing taste of the 50 per cent of women who like soap opera, the advertiser failed utterly to put anything on the air to appeal to the 50 per cent of women who hated it. Their radios stayed off all day; radio lost more than half of its daytime audience and ruined its daytime programming structure.

If television is not to follow this path which, in the long run, is ruinous to its own best interests, it must run its own shop. In this regard it is encouraging to note that the Columbia Broadcasting System, in its 1949 year-end report, revealed that the network owned more than 30 hours of its 45 hours a week of network TV shows. There are many other signs that television will be far less subservient to the advertiser than was radio. The extent of that subservience is best illustrated by a story M. H. Aylesworth, first president of NBC, tells on himself. Years ago Aylesworth, the most important executive in broadcasting at the time, used to dance—actually dance—to the piping of the president of the American Tobacco Company. The late George Washington Hill used to drop in to his office while the Lucky Strike Dance Orchestra was on the air and make Aylesworth dance with a feminine member of the NBC staff to make sure the tempo was right for dancing. It is doubtful whether William S. Paley would submit to such an indignity today. And it's high time.

2) Radio never fully exploited its enormous potentialities

Back in the 1920's, Secretary of Commerce Herbert Hoover hailed radio as the greatest potential purveyor of news, music, culture, education and entertainment of all time. But radio never lived up to this bright promise. Its growth was stunted by the success of a few formulas: the big comedians like Jack Benny; the family comedy like Henry Aldrich; the soap opera; the whodunit; the audience-participation show; the dramatization of successful movies; the quiz show; and so on. Five hours of soap opera in the daytime and four hours—block programming is the official name for it—of whodunits at night. Amnesia in the afternoon and death in the evening. Radio did its best to make neurotics out of a whole generation of housewives with its soap operas alone, an endless succession of unfortunate heroines stricken with hysterical blindness. Hysterical blindness, incidentally, is one of the rarest ailments known to mankind but, at one time, half of the soap-opera heroines on the air came down with it at once as if it were measles. (One of them contracted it by eating chocolate cake.)

The lack of balance in radio's programming, however, is not so much of a sin of commission as one of omission. Radio's contribution to education, from which so much was expected, was practically nonexistent. The best the broadcaster could do was to plant four intellectuals around a table. One of them would lift a forefinger and say, "I think." The man across the table would lift his forefinger and say, "I disagree." Whenever he was accused of neglecting—some critics went so far as to accuse him of debasing—the culture of his country, the broadcaster retorted that he had broadcast at one time or another virtually all the world's great books and plays. He had, too—usually around midnight when the clientele was in bed.

It is depressing to note that television has already gone hog-wild over one formula—the vaudeville show. . . .

Television is a far more versatile medium than radio and too important a national asset to be given over exclusively to soft-shoe routines. The television broadcaster should determine in his own mind the importance—not the popularity but the *importance*—of the various types of programs he is capable of presenting. One of the most popular features of a newspaper is the comic strip, but no editor would dream of filling the whole newspaper with them.

3) Radio consistently pandered to the lowest tastes and almost ignored the highest

As a mass medium radio had to try to please all sorts of ages and incomes and cultural levels at the same time. . . . It aimed so diligently at the lowest common denominator of society that it never squarely hit any level at all.

By so conducting its operations, radio earned the contempt of the educated and cultivated people of the land. This comparatively small group exerts an influence far out of proportion to its numbers. These people, whom radio ignored, own and operate industry. They edit the newspapers. They write the books and plays. They imprinted their scorn on *all* levels of society. And, while the American people listened to radio in vast numbers, they never quite respected it.

To get rid of this regrettable heritage, the TV broadcaster should call attention to the fact that he has put on the air many things besides Hopalong Cassidy. He ought to remind the folks that he has televised *Julius Caesar, Macbeth, The Scarlet Letter, The Dybbuk, The Copperhead, Dear Brutus, The Comedy of Errors, Wuthering Heights, Barchester Towers* and scores of the greatest books and plays of all time. Neither the stage nor the movies can claim so distinguished a roster in so short a space of time. Yet television is considered a moronic form of entertainment simply because it became fashionable to regard any form of broadcasting as moronic, which shows how dangerous it is to ignore the minority groups of the American public.

4) Radio was morally irresponsible to the American people

Television is either going to elevate American tastes—or it's going to debase them. It's not going to leave them alone. The radio broadcaster, prodded from behind by a slick public-relations man, used to protest that radio was the mirror of the American people; that, if you criticized radio, you criticized the American people. It was a very clever and very specious argument. But it was not the responsibility of the listener to request something he had never heard of. It was radio's—and it is now television's—responsibility to improve its own product. Granted that the competitive situation was different, the automobile industry didn't produce the self-starter only after it was suggested by a disgruntled automobile buyer. Similarly the housewife is not going to outline for the benefit of the TV industry any bright new ideas for a television program. The industry will have to do its own creative thinking.

Radio derived enormous, and I think wholly false, satisfaction from counting heads and assuming unwarrantably that they were contented heads. No matter what television puts on the air, it is going to have an enormous audience, and the TV broadcaster had better not mistake this fact—as did the radio broadcaster—as automatic proof that he is doing a wonderful job. Every TV program will inform or educate or morally elevate or emotionally stimulate a lot of people. Or it will deceive or degrade or hypnotize them. It won't leave them unscathed. The broadcaster's responsibility therefore is an imposing one. He should judge every one of his programs—as well as his over-all program structure—with one thing in mind: it will do a great many people some good or it will do a great many people some harm.

In order to do this, television must develop some personal standards of excellence, which is something radio never did. Radio borrowed its standards from other media and, in those cases where there weren't any earlier standards to fall back on, it didn't have any. According to this method of operation, a great radio play was simply the dramatization of a good movie, a good book or a good play. Some of the best radio dramas were written solely for radio but because they had not received the prior endorsement of a book, a movie or a theatre critic, the industry looked down upon them as not quite respectable. If television is ever to amount to anything of cultural importance, it should rid itself of the idea that it's the motion picture industry, the book business or the stage. It's a big, new art form of its own. It was radio's lack of standards that led to that dizzy lunacy known as the giveaway program. Radio programs gave away washing machines, Cadillacs, $1,000 bills, houses—everything, in fact. . . .

5) Radio was avaricious

A man who wants to start a newspaper or magazine—and has enough money to do it—starts one and keeps it going as long as the public wants it. If he wants to start a radio station, though, it's different. Radio stations are limited by the number of broadcasting frequencies. And by the law established in 1934 the FCC allots those frequencies "in the public interest, convenience or necessity." The FCC doesn't *give* the broadcasters those frequencies; each station is merely loaned the frequency on its promise to use it in the best interests of the listeners who are its real owners. That's the law, but you wouldn't know it from listening to the radio. While a few stations, such as New York City's WNYC and many of the 100-odd educational stations, are publicly owned, the vast majority of stations are privately owned and operated. And although these stations have their frequencies on loan, they seem to regard them in the same manner as they do the microphones and the washrooms. The promises made to FCC by the applicants for frequencies make very funny reading in the light of their subsequent performances. In fact, for all practical purposes, the broadcaster does own his frequency, once he has gotten it.

Many sizable fortunes were made in radio. In 24 years the advertiser poured billions of dollars into radio. Where did it go? Well, let's take the $500 million annual income and slice it up. In the first place, 15 per cent of it, or $75 million, went into the pockets of the advertising agencies. . . . Now what did the advertising men do to earn that $75 million? Well, a lot of them worked very hard for it, of course, assembling the whole show. But there is also a very pleasant way to "assemble a show" that quickly became popular. This method, which now constitutes about 15 per cent of the programs, is the package deal. Rather than strain his own mind producing a show, the advertiser simply found a package producer. If the package happened to be *Information Please,* he paid as much as $11,000 a week for what cost its owner, Dan Golenpaul, from $5,000 to $7,500 to produce. For consummating this deal the ad-man made about 15 per cent of the cost, or $64,350 for the year—a 39-week year. He didn't net this, of course, because he had to pay out a lot of it for such things as his fixed expenses, liaison between the package producer and the sponsor and advertising the program. Just the same, say he grossed $64,350. That's still an awfully nice gross.

Young couples like Dorothy Kilgallen and Dick Kollmar cleared as much as $100 thousand a year for chattering over their breakfast cups about the people they'd seen the night before. . . . The offices of network vice presidents began to look like something out of the Palazzo Venezia, and network presidents, in order to be properly differentiated from their vice presidents, had to add wainscoted private dining rooms with their own kitchens. There would be nothing especially wrong with this opulence, but radio, after all, is a semipublic institution, so it has a responsibility to the public to produce at least some programs that are in the best interests of the public.

Both the advertiser and the broadcaster had plenty of money to put a new idea or a new personality on the air and keep it there until the public accepted it. Rarely was this done. The old faces—the Jack Bennys and Fred Allens and Amos 'n' Andys—got richer, and there were no new faces and no new ideas. In the end this dollar worship proved almost disastrous. When Jack Benny was lured from NBC to CBS by the promise of more dollars (2.3 million of them, to be exact), NBC's entire program structure almost fell apart. . . .

6) Radio created an insulting picture of the American people

The broadcaster and the advertising man never got to know the American people very well. They genuflected to the most clamorous and idiotic elements of America. The letter writers, for example. Mae West once appeared on the Charlie McCarthy program and let fly a few remarks which appeared to be out of bounds. The repercussion shook NBC to its foundations. Yet when the smoke had cleared away it developed that only 15,000 persons, not all of them angry, had written in about the broadcast—out of an audience of roughly 20 million. It was difficult to explain to the broadcaster that most Americans don't write letters. They turn the . . . thing off and go bowling.

Then there was the studio audience—Americans all—who shrieked with laughter and applauded like maniacs at the most feeble witticisms. After all, they had been let in free and they were encouraged and, in some cases, almost forced to show their appreciation. The studio audience was brought into radio by Ed Wynn, and Eddie Cantor, a couple of veterans of the stage, who couldn't function without it. Immediately the subtleties of the pioneer radio comedians—Stoopnagle and Budd and the early audienceless *Amos' 'n' Andy*—were drowned in a torrent of bof-folos which were provoked by a much lower level of humor. The introduction of this audience which stood between the entertainer and his real audience—two or three people in a living room— was one of the most lamentable mistakes ever made by radio.

Another reason why radio so profoundly misunderstood the American people can be ascribed to its points of origin. At the start some of the best radio programs emanated from Chicago, Cincinnati and a host of other communities. When radio grew rich and successful it settled immovably in New York and Hollywood, two of the least characteristic cities in the country. . . . About 70 per cent of the costliest and most important programs emanated from Hollywood, a city so far removed from the main stream of American life that the listener had to have a special frame of reference to understand the jokes. The smog; the irresponsibility of the Los Angeles motorists; Cucamonga. That was the stuff of which radio spun its dreams. It was not only trivia; it was *local* trivia.

Television is still young and some of its best programs are coming from Chicago, Philadelphia and Washington—as well as from New York and Hollywood. It would be to television's best interests, to say nothing of ours, if a fair share of its programs came from and represented all parts of the country. Above all, television shouldn't spend too much time in southern California. . . .

7) *Radio was cowardly*

. . . Rich and influential as was radio, it was the most timid medium of them all. Radio was afraid to offend the Negroes, the Irish, the Jews or the Women's Bowling League of East Orange, N.J. Hugh Johnson wasn't allowed to broadcast a script that discussed syphilis for fear it might ruffle the sensibilities of some bluenose society. General Johnson wasn't *for* syphilis, either. . . .

Politeness is all very well but the thing can be carried too far. Sheer inoffensiveness is so small a virtue as to be no virtue at all. No one ever accomplished anything in this world without stepping on somebody's toes. The FCC has now given the broadcaster the right to harbor opinions. . . . Fellows, harbor some and hold to them. There are many times when the American people need and deserve censure. Go ahead and censure them. No man will turn you off. He'll think you're talking about the man next door.

Radio's timidity colored most of its programs. "Here is Joe Doakes, your friendly announcer." "The voice with the smile." "And here is your host." "Your friend and mine." For heaven's sake, television, don't be so friendly to just everybody. Lots of people aren't entitled to your friendship. Don't play host to everyone who comes along and don't smile *all* the time. There are times when the voice with a scowl is more appropriate and far more courageous.

One final word. Just because I dwelt at such length on radio's faults, I'd like to make it clear that I am not unaware of radio's virtues. It has many of them. But this, after all, is about radio's Seven Deadly Sins.

TV TRIES A NEW TACK [4]

Robert E. Sherwood, winner of three Pulitzer prizes for drama and one for biography, has signed a contract with the National Broadcasting Company to write nine original plays for television. The first will be seen in the spring [of 1953].

Under the contract Mr. Sherwood is assured of greater financial reward and greater artistic freedom than ever have been granted a writer in the field of broadcasting. His minimum guarantee for the nine plays, exclusive of all subsequent royalties, will run to six figures. For each script his compensation will exceed the largest fee ever paid a Hollywood star for a single television performance.

A stipulation in the contract, said to be the first of its kind in either radio or television, expressly relieves Mr. Sherwood of any requirement to confer with representatives of commercial sponsors or advertising agencies. The pact provides further that he need not deal with more than one key executive at NBC. The choice of subject matter for the dramas, each of which is to be

[4] From "Sherwood to Pen Nine TV Plays," by Jack Gould, Radio-Television Editor, New York *Times*. New York *Times*. p 1+. November 24, 1952. Reprinted by permission.

of an hour's duration, is left entirely to him. The only theme
that is barred is religious controversy.

Frank M. Folsom, president of the Radio Corporation of
America, parent company of NBC, and Mr. Sherwood agreed
the contract had significant ramifications in the artistic development of television.

Mr. Folsom attached special importance to the decision of
a writer of Mr. Sherwood's stature to work on a regular basis in
television, and expressed the hope that he would be followed by
many other leading playwrights. He added that NBC was happy
to grant Mr. Sherwood the artistic freedom, which, he said, "all
fine authors require to create great works of art."

Mr. Sherwood said he believed the contract constituted recognition by NBC that television must be creative in its own right
and could not rely for its dramatic material on outside sources,
such as best sellers, magazine stories, Broadway plays and movie
scripts. He stressed that heretofore a writer in broadcasting had
had to work in what he called a "no-man's land" of sponsors,
advertising agencies, package producers and minor network func-
tionaries. Now, he said, a precedent has been set for the policy
makers of a broadcasting company to deal directly with an author.

Failure of Hollywood executives to establish a direct business
relationship with the writer and recognize the importance of his
independence, Mr. Sherwood said, thwarted the cultural growth
of the motion picture industry for many years. . . .

Mr. Sherwood's plays are intended for commercial sponsorship on the air. The playwright made it clear that, in insisting
on freedom from sponsor interference or control, he was moti-
vated by what he believed were the best interests of both the
creative writer and the advertiser.

"When you are dealing with sponsors and advertising agencies," he explained, "you are dealing with people whose primary
interest is not what you write in television. Their primary interest is in selling their product. We want to do the best possible
work on NBC television and, having done that, let the sponsor
come along."

Separation of the theatrical and advertising functions of television, he said, should lead to improved programming that would be advantageous to the sponsor.

Asserting that television's swelling audience provided a real challenge to the writer, he said that if the industry was now ready to offer dramatists both a measure of financial security and an opportunity to speak for themselves, many writers might choose to remain in New York rather than go to Hollywood. This, he suggested, might result in a number of dramatists resuming work in the theatre.

A RADIO "NEWSPAPER" [5]

Trouble with many a radio station is that it starts out on a soap opera and canned music formula, and never learns to get along on any other diet.

But that hasn't been the case with station WAVZ in New Haven, Conn. It has torn up the orthodox radio station menu [and] broken with the tradition of worshiping the almighty sponsor. . . .

It has done this by superimposing the personality of a newspaper upon the body and framework of radio.

This 1000-watt, daytime-only station lives on news. Every day it puts on the air the equivalent of a complete 10-page newspaper. The station boasts reporters, a city editor, a city desk. It "covers" every story in town, in competition with the newspapers. The major difference is that it's often hours ahead of the newspapers.

The reporters carry pencil and pad, just like other reporters. They interview. They get the facts. They build up the "news angle." One thing is different, however. These reporters must record as well as report. They carry with them portable tape recorders with which they preserve the sounds and excitement of every news event.

If there's a fire in town, the listener hears not only the reporter's account of the fire. He also hears the fire engines, listens

[5] From "The Radio Station That Dares to Be Different." *Changing Times.* p32-3. November 1950. Reprinted by permission.

to the excited comments of fire fighters or bystanders, maybe even gets an earful of the tale of the fire's distraught victims.

Once, when a four-year-old boy disappeared, searchers combed the countryside for four days. WAVZ reporters tramped right along, followed the leads, interviewed exhausted friends and relatives of the boy. Here was all the drama and color of the search, set down not in drab prose, but in its real-life context. Listeners were avid for details and followed the story with all the suspense of someone on the scene. When the little boy was finally found, drowned in a lake, the emotional impact was so great that listeners wept when they called the station to get further details.

A newspaper, however, has special features in addition to straight news, and this radio-newspaper follows suit. It presents society events, book and theatre reviews, sports news. It encourages letters to the editor. Want ads, marriage and birth announcements, obituaries—even comics—fill out the program.

All this takes a staff of six newspaper reporters turned radio reporters to keep the "paper" on the air. It also takes a considerable amount of gumption on the part of the two ex-newsmen who, not knowing a thing about radio, decided to flout radio's hoary traditions by making WAVZ a newspaper of the air.

Victor W. Knauth originated the idea of this "living newspaper." For nine years, Knauth had wrestled with his conscience over his decision in 1940 to sell out as publisher of the *Times-Star,* a Bridgeport, Conn., paper. The buyer was the competing local paper.

"Economically the sale made sense," Knauth now confesses. "But to the community it meant a newspaper monopoly, with one point of view, one publisher, and not much incentive for reporters to 'compete' for the story."

Knauth felt that there must be another way to give the public the news without spending the hundreds of thousands of dollars required to run a good-sized daily newspaper. Radio, he decided, was the answer, or at least the nearest thing to an answer that could be got at the fraction of the $600 thousand it had taken to run the *Times-Star.*

Small radio stations can be had for under $75 thousand. The cost of operation never approaches the overhead of a newspaper. For one thing, no presses to operate and pay for. For another, no linotype machines. And there is no delivery problem, no newsprint to buy, none of the day-to-day problems of deciding how big or small the newspaper is to be.

It wasn't until he met another newsman, Daniel W. Kops, that Knauth's idea materialized. With Kops, he purchased WAVZ, then a run-of-the-mill station with a shaky future, at best.

Knauth and Kops spent the first three months "rehearsing in public," as Knauth puts it. Not the least of their problems was ridding reporters of their "deadline" mentality. And ridding announcers of long-practiced routines.

Reporters were taught to consider "press time" as far away as the nearest telephone, and within the next five minutes. Announcers were taught to "get cozy with the audience, a little colloquial with their language" if they were to be warm and intimate with their listeners. . . .

WAVZ's advertisers are mainly neighborhood shops which can't afford to use newspapers—florists, dairies, taverns, tire dealers, music stores, and the like. The ads are basically the "spot" kind, those 30-second or 60-second announcements offered to the listener along with news. There are no 15-minute or half-hour shows under the sponsorship of one advertiser. Knauth says that policy keeps the station "editorially independent."

The station is not averse to showing its civic muscles whenever it thinks it necessary. Two-minute editorials are a frequent part of its listeners' menu. They cover everything from politics to national defense. And WAVZ is not afraid to put on special campaigns.

City officials at one time dilly-dallied for nine months over the sale of a tract of land wanted by the State Housing Authority for veterans' housing. A municipal piggery occupied the site, and the authorities were averse to moving it.

"What does New Haven want—pigs or people?" demanded WAVZ. To show the contrast, the station put house-hungry veterans on the air five times a day, alternating their comments with grunts of the pigs, tape-recorded on the site. In three days city officials got the point, and the vets are now getting their houses.

On another occasion, the station went to bat for the local Negro community which was getting nowhere in its campaign to replace a 75-year-old schoolhouse with a new one. WAVZ dramatized the situation on the air, taking listeners right into the school by means of tape recordings. The new school is now on its way.

As Knauth shrewdly observes, the main competition for the station is not the other radio stations as much as the two local newspapers, the *Register* and the *Journal-Courier*. Both are owned by publisher John Day Jackson.

"We compete for news, not very often for ads," says Knauth.

The competition for news sometimes gets a little rough. Relations are not at the breaking point, but the papers maintain a studied indifference to WAVZ as well as to other local stations. No local radio programs are printed in the papers—a situation by no means unique to New Haven. WAVZ's campaigns are never mentioned. Its political position is ignored.

But for WAVZ, the newspapers do exist and are fair game for attack. . . . A favorite line of the station is "You won't see this in New Haven's newspapers, but. . . ."

Will all this pay off? Can radio dress up in the garb of the press and still make the most of its own special talents? Yes, say Knauth and Kops. They think there is something of the pioneer in WAVZ. It is primarily a dispenser of news and views, not a huckster of wares. To many listeners of many radio stations, that seems emphatically like pioneering.

HELPING HAND FROM THE FOUNDATIONS [6]

I saw a kinescope recently of a forty-minute TV program presented over WOI-TV, the only television station as yet owned and operated by an educational institution, Iowa State College. . . .

    [6] From "The World Floods into Iowa," by Robert Lewis Shayon, radio and television critic, *Saturday Review* and *Christian Science Monitor. Saturday Review.* 35:16+. September 13, 1952. Reprinted by permission.

"Question Before the House," a one-time telecast, discussed the emotions and decisions faced by boys of draft age when the time comes for them to enter military service. "Discussed" is the official word: the program was produced with money granted by the Fund for Adult Education, established by the Ford Foundation, expressly for pilot work in community level TV discussion programs. But this was no ordinary "discussion."

Essayed by Mayo Simon, producer, and Dick Hartzell, director, was a daring, imaginative experiment in mass therapy employing "role playing" (pretending to be somebody else and speaking his thoughts) and personnel counseling by people in identical, real situations. The producers wanted to say something meaningful to the people of Iowa about this going-into-the-service problem. With the assistance of the college's extension service and county agents, they probed the experiences and concerns of draft eligibles, their families, girl friends, veterans, draft-boards, etc. On the night of the telecast, 4-H clubs, Scout, church, farm, and other organizations were coordinated into an imposing network of local groups which watched the show and after it was over followed it with an off-the-air sharing of their own responses.

What they saw and heard was a rough, honest, and at times deeply moving articulation of the cross-currents of fear, resentment, resignation, hope, and affirmation that pull at American minds and hearts as the cold, shooting war in Korea and the encircling world tension continue to sear individual lives. Twenty-three representative Iowans gathered from ten counties to play the "roles."

"Question Before the House" was the defiant muzzle of a bold, new gun thrust into the face of dominant thinking and practice in American TV and radio. It said in effect: "We want to blow the lid off approaches, perhaps once valid but now stale with nonadventure. We want to dare to try novel techniques, dare to fail, to learn, to get out from the four husks of studio walls to where the people are—not the people that lose any semblance of what they are when they walk into stereotype formulas, but the people as they really are in their prejudices, angers, strengths, shortcomings, and magnificent potential for awareness and action."

This program would never have faced a lens but for the role another Ford Foundation agency, the Fund for the Advancement of Education, is playing in radio-TV. Early this year at Iowa State, FAE money made possible the experimental series, "The Whole Town's Talking," 16 programs, 30 minutes to an hour in length, in which Iowans came to grips with deep-lying community controversies between the two poles of problem-facing and decision-making. I know something about these programs, for I produced and directed the first seven.

Not only were they innovations in discussion techniques; to all who shared them, they were glimpses of democratic behavior integrating campus, university extension, TV, state, town, and county government, the people, and the press. Iowans on the air met and wrestled not with social, political and economic abstractions over which they have small control, but with such specific, manageable town and county issues as school district reorganization, municipal water-systems, rebuilding county courthouses, teen-age recreation centers, etc. They proved that given the opportunity (which in this instance TV provided) they can speak up, dissent, vote, clarify the public mind, and move or not move as they see fit. And they did it with integrity, intelligence, authentic American forensic and—networks please note—sophistication and wit.

Were it not for grants from the Ford Foundation, the Joint Committee on Educational TV would not have been set up and adequately financed to spearhead the campaign which resulted in the Federal Communications Commission's setting aside of channels for future noncommercial license applicants. And now the JCET, with further grants, is working to help educators employ those reserved channels usefully.

In radio, Ford money has enabled the National Association of Educational Broadcasters to organize, extend, and promote their tape network sharing BBC, CBC, Australian, and some American exchange features. Beginning . . . [in September 1952] the first series of NAEB-produced shows, Ford-financed, . . .

were broadcast by] some forty of the network's stations. "The Jeffersonian Heritage," starring Claude Rains, is . . . based on the research, writing, and advice of Professor Dumas Malone of the Department of History of Columbia University. Its goal is to "reflect the American ideology as Jefferson saw it . . . [that] human considerations come first and the sanctity of the personality and freedom of the mind are the most precious of human possessions." . . .

"Ways of Mankind," a series of anthropology broadcasts, . . . [has been] produced for the NAEB by the Canadian Broadcasting Corporation. . . . Another ambitious undertaking [is] "People Under Communism," full-hour broadcasts "based on documented evidence and expert knowledge about the power and intentions of the Soviet Union." This series is produced "in consultation with scholars from the Russian Institute of Columbia University, the Russian Research Center at Harvard University, and the Hoover Institute and Library at Stanford University." . . .

At last we have in America the beginnings of broadcast production permanently free from the debilitating exigencies which hound the networks' torturous struggle with culture. We are no longer transcription colonies of the BBC; the time has come to show what we can do. . . .

On the record to date it is Ford . . . that has made the big push in adult education via radio and TV. And of that push, the exploration, the willingness to speak, as the NAEB puts it, to "thinking Americans," has been in the educational field. Much could be said about some of the weaknesses of the foundation's approach to radio and TV, its still fragmentary nature, its apparent lack of a total, courageous vision of the possibilities of the media. There has been internecine strife between the commercial and educational arms; and open to strong dissent is the foundation's avowed policy of "seeking out, encouraging, and extending suitable existing activities wherever possible and bringing into being new activities only where necessary." Existing activities are often more suitable to their own interests and ambitions rather than to long-range educational aims.

In this respect, the record is unequivocally clear: remove the Fund for Adult Education from the present radio-TV structure, and with one blow you remove the only current, affirmative hope for improving the cultural tone of this widely influential American medium.

BROADCASTING AS A COMMUNITY ENTERPRISE [7]

Station WNYC [owned and operated by the City of New York] is America's foremost noncommercial radio station. . . .

Few will deny the value of the outstanding cultural and recreational programs of WNYC, but many . . . who recognize in radio a powerful medium for developing cooperation between the citizen and his government will ask a few practical questions along this line: How useful was WNYC . . . in providing better government? Was it worth $235,155 a year or $17.57 an hour of program service to eight million people? What kind of a public-relations job did it do for department heads and the city?

The Administrative Code of the City of New York . . . provides that the facilities of the Municipal Broadcasting System "may be used as an adjunct to any municipal agency which may require or use such service." . . .

Among the more frequent users were the Departments of Markets, Health, Hospitals, Water Supply, and Sanitation. The program material may be worked out from raw notes provided by the department to the station, or it may be a joint effort, but in many instances it is the creation of the department concerned. For example, every morning three employees of the Department of Markets arrive at the station ready to give the housewives the "best buys" of the day. . . .

During the water shortage of late 1949 and early 1950, the Department of Water Supply went on the air to take the message of conservation right into the consumer's home. Their "plugs" and spot announcements, together with the dramatic presentation

[7] From "WNYC," by Irving Luscombe, Lecturer in History, Newark College of Rutgers University. *American City.* 65:136-7. December 1950. Reprinted by permission.

of the facts of water storage, consumption, and comparison with previous years' totals, are credited with having aided the city in winning the battle of water.

The Department of Hospitals has used the facilities of the municipal radio station frequently to direct the attention of young women to the value, service, and satisfaction in a nursing career.

The Department of Sanitation is enlisting the efforts of block-residents by arousing pride in their neighborhood. Cooperating in this effort are the New York *Herald Tribune,* the Police Department and their PAL (Police Athletic League) groups. . . . Attention of the listeners is directed to the need for a city-wide block-by-block clean-up. They are reminded that in a program entitled *The Block of the Week,* on Saturday mornings at ten-thirty, the station honors those whose block was selected as the best example of cooperative cleaning. At the same time the *Herald Tribune* sponsors a contest offering a prize of $500 to the PAL unit doing the best job of cleaning up its block. . . .

Utilization of the municipal radio station is offered not only to official agencies, but also to nongovernment groups and organizations. Over 700 nonprofit social, welfare, and public-service agencies requested (and received) the use of the radio facilities of WNYC and WNYC-FM. A listing of such organizations shows colleges, housing developments, foundations, all religious charitable groups, the Veterans Administration, and hundreds of others, covering every phase of city life.

In metropolitan centers, minorities tend to be large, active, and vocal. They demand special services. WNYC has served them generously and well.

These are anxious days for those in reserve outfits [and in service]. Their interests are cared for by the "Armed Forces Newsreel," a program emanating from a private wire direct to Military Services Headquarters. Special news bulletins affecting thousands of reservists are broadcast as soon as announced. Veterans' Service programs answer important questions and clarify confusing points regarding GI Bill privileges.

The contributions of WNYC and WNYE in the field of radio education are quite well known. (WNYE is the Board of Education's separate FM station which broadcasts special pro-

grams to the city's 900 schools.) Not so well known, but of great
importance as a pioneering effort in the use of FM for the
advancement of medical education, is the *Post Graduate Radio
Program* of the New York Academy of Medicine. Once a week
over WNYC-FM . . . the Academy has presented a lecture on the
latest medical information by outstanding authorities. These
lectures are not for the laity, but are directed especially to medical
men.

Although there are no channels available at this time for a
municipal television station in the New York region, the city
station has created a Television Film Unit to translate government in terms of the new medium. . . .

Among WNYC's outstanding public-service programs are the
"gavel-to-gavel" broadcasts of the United Nations' sessions,
which have been given greater coverage by WNYC than by any
other radio station in America. . . .

One of the happy by-products of its practice of recording all
important speeches given over WNYC is a growing collection of
the voices of the world's most eminent men. . . .

Throughout its history, WNYC has catered to the needs of
the moment of New York citizens. Its programs have been designed to help them in prosperity, depression, war, inflation,
and periods of panic-buying. This policy has helped "nearly
eight million Americans live together in peace and harmony and
enjoy the benefits of democracy," a phrase often used in identi-
fying WNYC over the air-waves.

CO-OP BROADCASTING [8]

Washington [D. C.] can boast . . . [a] pioneering institution—a listener-owned radio station. This is station WCFM,
owned and operated as a consumers' cooperative. . . .

WCFM has proved itself a real community institution. When
they want to be heard over Washington families' radio sets, all
sorts of groups turn to WCFM. Among these are the local co-

⁸ From "Listeners' Radio—Why Not?" by former Representative Jerry Voorhis
(Democrat, California), leader in cooperative movements in the United States. *Survey.*
87:259-61. June 1951. Reprinted by permission.

operatives including the first consumer-owned department store, Group Health Association, the District credit union movement, and the Greenbelt [Maryland, housing development] shopping center. But they also include citizens' associations, the League of Women Voters, United World Federalists, and other civic organizations. AFL and CIO unions often broadcast programs of public interest, and several unions regularly sponsor programs of news commentary. High school and college groups appear frequently—in programs ranging from sports commentary and drama to the "I Speak for Democracy" oratorical contest. Churches of all denominations broadcast their messages over this station.

When the idea of a cooperatively owned radio station first was discussed, during World War II, it was called a utopian dream. A group of consumers' cooperative enthusiasts, led by WCFM's first manager, Helmuth Kern, were working on postwar blueprints for Potomac area cooperatives. As one of the group's major projects, they set to work to organize a radio station, broadcasting on the lower-cost and higher-quality FM band.

In the discussion and planning stages, the guiding idea was to include a great variety of community groups, from the labor unions to the League of Women Voters. Washingtonians, whose city council is the United States Congress, have no franchise. Therefore, these voluntary organizations take on many of the aspects of spokesmen for the community. When it came time to put up the initial capital, many of these groups were unable to assume responsibility, and the station was capitalized primarily by the local cooperatives, and by purchase of stock by individuals. However, there has been no major change in the original program plans, and these groups still actively participate in preparing and broadcasting programs over WCFM. But the station has never been adequately capitalized and has in consequence faced severe financial problems. . . .

The mere fact that it has survived is noteworthy, because the mortality rate of FM stations has been very high even where they have had the advantage of substantial capital. By commercial standards, it is making progress, having attracted such national sponsors of its programs as Kaiser-Frazer, the Welch Grape

Juice Company, and the Farm Bureau Insurance Companies, not to mention a growing group of local advertisers who find WCFM listeners the kind of people who show appreciation for advertising over *their* station in the most practical of ways—by purchases of goods and services.

Needless to say, the going has not been easy. Costs doubled between the day WCFM's application was filed with the Federal Communications Commission and the day it went on the air. . . .

Most of WCFM's capital has been subscribed by the more than 2700 individuals who hold shares of its preferred stock selling at $10 a share. These are the people from every walk of life and many parts of the country who have made continuance of the station possible. In addition, the basic controlling group of Washington cooperatives owns the common stock on behalf of twenty-five thousand members. . . .

The scarcity of commercials on WCFM has its virtues, but also drawbacks. Obviously, no station can operate on good will alone. WCFM is competing with more than a dozen other stations in the area. Its monthly budget is about $6500; the station's advertising income, although increasing steadily, is nothing like enough to meet that cost. A normally run station, under such circumstances, would have only two alternatives—to fold up, or to sell spot commercials at five-minute intervals, accept any advertising accompanied by cash, and consequently operate the station with little concern for the listening audience.

To solve this most pressing problem of filling its income gap, WCFM's management played around with a number of methods. They explored "functional music" production for offices, restaurants, and places of business. This and several other ideas were rejected on the ground that they do not represent good radio programming.

Instead, a growing and thriving record-producing business has been developed which promises to play a major part in reducing the amount of red ink used by the station's book-keeper. . . .

Another important by-product of WCFM's search for income —and for more nearly capacity use of its ample facilities and competent engineering staff—has been a recording business for advertising agencies and the many organizations which send "platters" out from Washington to their local units. The Democratic National Committee has made extensive use of WCFM for campaign recordings. The Food and Agricultural Organization [of the United Nations] also uses the studio's recording facilities, as do several Washington advertising agencies.

Another related function has been the servicing that WCFM provides for other radio stations. . . . Many of WCFM's special events broadcasts are purchased for reuse on stations which have no network connection in Washington.

Senators, congressmen, and administrative officials, as well as hundreds of civil servants who make up the bulk of Washington's population, own stock in WCFM. . . .

One clue to the kind of people who support WCFM can be seen in the make-up of its recently chosen board. Not one is a professional radio man. The group includes Wallace Campbell, who finds time from his duties as Washington representative of the Cooperative League of the USA to serve as board chairman, C. Edward Behre, an official of the Forestry Service, and Paul R. Porter, [formerly] Assistant Administrator of ECA; also a high school teacher, an official of a private employment agency, an attorney at the United States Patent Office, a public relations man for the Rural Electrification Administration, the editor of the AFL Machinists' weekly paper, all are on the governing body, along with the economist, Robert Nathan, Tilford Dudley, assistant director of CIO-PAC, Mary Anderson, the retired chief of the United States Women's Bureau, and Benjamin Segal, former local chairman of Americans for Democratic Action.

There have been questions—really touchy questions—of programming for WCFM. Take the matter of accepting liquor advertising, for instance. The board had laid down a general policy statement on accepting only advertising that was in good taste. After a flood of protests greeted a beer commercial, the board discussed and restated that policy: no liquor ads, no beer ads, no patent medicine ads.

Or, take the question of religious broadcasts. One of the most lucrative sources of income of many small radio stations is paid time for evangelistic broadcasts. The listeners' committee of WCFM and the board decided originally to set aside time each week for free broadcasts of religious programs, arranging to share the time among all the denominations which cared to use the station. Then an enterprising minister liked the response from WCFM listeners so much that he offered to purchase time regularly for his messages. The board decided to try this, and the program was put on the air for a frankly experimental period. Listener reaction generally was unfavorable—not because they found the particular program objectionable, but because they did not want a precedent set. So the paid program was dropped, and all religious broadcasts are again on free time.

The listeners' council, which is named by the board from among the stockholders, has direct influence upon the station's programs. The council moves into action when complaints are made, or when a challenging new program idea is presented. Ask a WCFM owner-listener what he likes about his station, and you are likely to get one or more of these answers:

1. *The commentators.* WCFM is located at the news center of the world. It uses this fact to good advantage. A battery of eight news commentators can be heard each week on the station. They include columnists like Marquis Childs and Doris Fleeson, AFL-sponsored Frank Edwards, Joseph C. Harsch of the *Christian Science Monitor*, Mrs. Raymond Clapper, two labor experts —John Herling and Will Allen—Wallace Campbell of the Cooperative League, and the economist, Robert Nathan. In addition to these commentators, who speak precisely as they please without any sort of station censorship, WCFM schedules 32 minutes of news reports out of the six hours each day that the station is on the air.

2. *The music.* WCFM has pioneered in bringing "live" music back to Washington radio listeners. Previously, there had been only some brief broadcasts of the National Symphony Orchestra from high school auditoriums, and a winter series of good chamber music recitals broadcast from the Library of Congress. Last fall, in cooperation with the American Federation of Musicians, WCFM initiated a series of weekly chamber music broadcasts from its own studios. For some time, the station has

aired the Sunday night concerts from the National Gallery of Art. It features each Sunday evening a program of organ music and another of church choirs. Dr. William Ober, a trustee of the Haydn Society, and by profession a pathologist for the Army medical research program, comments on and plays rarely-heard classical music for ninety minutes each Saturday evening. His program follows closely that of Dr. Walter Kaplan, who performs the same rites for "Hot House Jazz."

3. *Events of public interest.* This is another pioneering venture of WCFM—the preparation of half-hour condensations of some of the many meetings, congressional hearings, and press conferences that take place in Washington. "Many historians," points out the program director, Jean Putnam, "have noted that, since the earliest days of America, both education and influence in our country have stemmed to a unique degree from the many powerful voluntary organizations of America.

"Washington is known as a convention city for such organizations. The most influential men in Congress and the government customarily speak before such organizations. Only in exceptional cases are these meetings given radio coverage, and even then only single speeches, without their audience background, are apt to be carried on the air." So WCFM records the whole event —frequently a full day's convention session—and then its program and engineering staff literally "snip and paste" the tape recording into a half-hour program which skillfully conveys the atmosphere and temper of the gathering. This technique has been used to "cover" such events as the all-day service at the Washington Cathedral on "God, Man, and the Hydrogen Bomb"; conventions of B'nai B'rith, Americans for Democratic Action, the National Forestry Association, and the American Newspaper Guild; a conference of the Food and Agricultural Organization of the UN; the all-day school of the League of Women Voters; and the Conference on Problems of the Aging, staged by the Federal Security Agency.

In addition to these three major attractions for listeners, the station offers regularly scheduled reports for consumers, a weekly review of drama by the newspaper critic, Tom Donnelly; "Religion Makes News" by the Reverend Thomas Keehn; explanations of Supreme Court decisions; and a fifteen-minute weekly program on the United Nations prepared in interview form by Mrs. Henry Holt, Jr.

The small fry are loyal followers of "Big Sister Sheila." Sheila Goldstein started telling stories into WCFM's microphones only a few months after the station went on the air, when she herself was only fourteen. Now, she is the proud possessor of a sponsor—Welch Grape Juice Company—and has a devoted audience of five- to eight-year-olds who often determine her stories by postcard requests.

To those who still envision city co-ops as confined to grocery stores, WCFM's story may come as something of a shock. But the story, whatever its final outcome, has already proved what men and women with vision, taste, and technical know-how can do through a cooperative venture aimed at meeting a real need of the consuming public.

THE ROLE OF ADVERTISING

EDITOR'S INTRODUCTION

In the history of broadcasting, there has been no stickier problem than that concerning the role of advertising. Commercial sponsorship of radio and television programs has been alternately blamed for broadcasting's shortcomings as a creative art and credited with its success as an industry.

Does the advertiser's responsibility to his product outweigh the broadcaster's responsibility (as determined by himself and Federal statute) to his audience? Or do both work together for the greater common good? As the articles in this section indicate, there are no easy answers.

It is not within the scope of this volume to examine in detail the system used in other countries, particularly Britain, which substitutes a tax on set ownership for commercial sponsorship of programs. Despite the frequently heard criticism of the excesses of advertising, there seems to be little opposition by any sizable group to a continuation of commercial sponsorship for American broadcasting. But there are ways, it is suggested, in which the system can be modified and improved, and these are discussed in this section.

In connection with this, the reader is referred to the article on subscription television ("Pay as You Look") in the first section of this volume. Subscription television offers one possibility for television broadcasting without advertising sponsorship.

As an addendum to the discussion of advertising's role, there is a report on a new issue—the use of radio broadcasting, commercially sponsored, in public transportation vehicles. This has led to the appearance of the "captive" audience, those who cannot avoid listening whether they wish to or not.

BROADCASTING'S MAIN SOURCE
OF REVENUE [1]

American radio is supported for the most part by revenue from advertising, of which there are two types: network advertising and local advertising. About twenty-five agencies handle most of the $200 million spent annually for big network advertisers. Of the 241 national advertisers on the four national networks in 1949, five major advertising groups accounted for almost three quarters of the total network time sales. They were (1) food and food products, (2) toilet goods, (3) smoking materials, (4) drugs and remedies, and (5) soaps and cleaners. Procter and Gamble spent over $17 million, which represents almost twice as much as the next two advertisers combined.

When advertisers spend such sizable sums for advertising, it is not surprising that they tend to exercise considerable control over the content of the programs they sponsor. Advertisers are out for sales. They are interested that their message be carried to the largest number of potential buyers possible. The whole program is built around the commercial, the entertainment being calculated to induce the listener to stay with the program until the next commercial announcement. Advertisers by and large are not interested in the welfare or interests of minority groups or in the advancement of American culture or taste. One radio executive described "good taste" by saying: "We don't want anything that would be offensive. We don't want anything improper, that couldn't be heard in the home."

Such a point of view makes radio programming entirely subservient to the undiscriminating taste of the general public, with very little chance for improvement. Procter and Gamble probably has more to say about what the American public will hear than any other single organization in America. . . .

In 1946 the trade magazine *Broadcasting* queried radio station managers throughout the nation to determine what factors or agencies had most retarded the improvement of broadcasting.

[1] From "Radio and Television and Ethical Standards," by Frederick C. Gruber, Assistant Professor of Education, Chairman of the Radio Committee, University of Pennsylvania. *Annals of the American Academy of Political and Social Science.* 280:116-24. March 1952. Reprinted by permission.

The station managers overwhelmingly laid the blame at the doors of the advertising agencies and the sponsors. Yet by law, the licensees, not the advertisers who buy time, are entrusted with the responsibility of determining what we shall hear.

In order to correct these abuses the radio industry has drawn up a great many restrictive rules. For example, the NAB *Standards of Practice* [2] suggests how much advertising time should be allowed for each broadcast period, that no advertising copy should be approved without positive proof of the truth of its statements, that the word "cure" should never be used in drug advertisements, that advertising copy should never be so placed that it could be mistaken for a news item, and that wherever possible the newscaster should not read the commercials. These suggestions, however, are negative in their approach, and many of them are constantly violated.

Bad as radio commercials may be, it must be said for the industry that they are generally of higher quality and veracity than the type of advertising permitted in the tabloid newspaper and the pulp magazine. Any comparison of press and radio advertising would show that considerably more care is used in the investigation of the claims of the product by radio program departments than is exercised by some types of publications.

It is not so much the commercials as the cheap quality of the fill-ins that offends the listeners. One step in the right direction, it seems, is the building of a balanced program by the network programming departments and the development by the networks and their affiliated stations of "package shows" [prepared as a unit in advance] which are offered for sale to sponsors at such times as fit into the program pattern. Such a practice will return the responsibility for programming to the broadcasters, where it legally belongs.

THE BROADCASTERS' "SENSE OF GUILT" [3]

Contemplating . . . the general flavor of licenses and franchises given out to broadcasters, I sense a pervading odor of the

[2] See selection from *Standards of Practice*, p153-9.—Ed.
[3] From *Listening*, by Albert N. Williams, radio writer, director, and critic. University of Denver Press. Denver. 1948. p71-7. Reprinted by permission.

doctrine of original sin about the industry, to which dogma both
the Federal Communications Commission and the industry appear
to subscribe.

It was first advanced in the early 1920's. . . . The Congress,
hurriedly having to organize a set of standards by which one of
several applicants for the same frequency could be chosen, cast
about for reliable yardsticks, and finding no precedent for the
misty business of sending words and music through the air, was
forced to invent its own measurements for fitness to engage in
this commerce.

Financial responsibility, personal integrity as attested by
absence of complaint, the applicant's standing in his community,
plus a relatively sense-making plan for programs seemed to be
the critical factors, and to this day they are adhered to.

However, all of these factors, important as they are, left one
matter unmentioned. This question, the most crucial, was the
matter of *intent*. It was more or less felt that some stewardship
should be set over an applicant's attitude and aims. Did he hope
to enter the radio business for the purpose of doing a little good
to a lot of people, or only to benefit himself?

It is the question that everybody has concerning every other
individual in the world. What's he up to?

Naturally, one cannot set measurements of accomplishment
before the fact. What the first commissioners finally did . . . was
to establish the doctrine that the air-waves can never belong to
any one person or corporation. In the present-day terminology
of the Federal Communications Commission . . . the idea is that
radio is not just another breed of private enterprise, but that
broadcasters are trustees for property belonging to the people of
the United States.

A secondary, though more specific, thesis of this dogma has
recently been advanced by the Commission in connection with
the proposed sales of certain radio stations. . . . The Commission
feels that it is somehow indicative of evil intent for a license-
holder to offer to sell his franchise and properties at a higher
price than the bare cost of the physical plant. It studiously
ignores the effort that the creation, through good programming,
of good will requires, and suspects any increase in value as

inherent in the franchise itself. . . . The entire relationship between broadcasters and the Commission is cluttered with semantic and ritualistic similarities to a wealthy and formal religion based on a sense of guilt.

Had the broadcasters originally denied the stigma of this sin, they might have made an interesting case on the following grounds—that the air is no more sacred than the ground, and that a franchise to convey words through the air is by no means different from a franchise to convey cabbages over the highways, or by rail. In those instances, the same problems of private use of, and profit from, public heritage obtain. And yet it is not only permitted, it is encouraged, that corporations shall profit by the increased value of the franchises they develop in the field of public utilities and interstate trade. Railroad companies are bought and sold with the blessings of a democracy-loving government, provided only that bankruptcy proceedings are not used to shelter schemers. Street-railway franchises can be marketed, steamship lines are privately owned and financially enjoyed, and airlines are notoriously active in investment markets where the only end is the increase in value through operation of the privilege of flying through the same air into which radio radiates.

It is a point of view that was never clearly tested in the early days when the ritual was first being distilled in the baffled minds of the men originally confronted with this intriguing new invention. It is too late now, perhaps, for a broadcaster to claim attention for that point of view in the courts, for unspoken laws are impossible of countervention—they are too formless and have no discernible limits.

And in addition, the broadcasters early accepted the implication that they were guilty of some obscure taint and should be required to prove themselves innocent at regular intervals. That acceptance served them in place of a conscience, and the past quarter century of broadcasting is merely the history of radio operators, network managers, and independent station owners wondering, not how useful to the public they can grow to be, but, rather, how commercial they dare to be.

They indicated, from the very start, that they would not attempt to take responsibility for the quality of the output of their stations, an absolute necessity if ever they were to test the validity of the first, vague formulations of national policy. They blithely turned over to advertisers and advertising agencies the program aspect of their operation. It was a candid admission that they expected to be put out of business at any time, for they made no effort to subsidize writers and performers, and to invest in the type of long-range thinking necessary to create out of the rough clay of radio a powerful and wise entertainment industry.

Radio is not, today, any of the things it was born to be. It is not operated primarily in the public interest. It is operated in the specific interest of certain patent medicine makers, soap chemists, and tobacco curers. It becomes an educational, political, and social force only after the salesmen have enjoyed their sport. Somebody has to fill up the remaining time, the hours when nobody is supposed to be listening, and radio might as well be a news organ and a public service at that time, particularly when such fare costs little or nothing to prepare.

Everybody knows the intent of a manufacturer. It is to sell as much of his product as he can. And the turning over of a selected thirty minutes of broadcast time to a manufacturer and his advertising agent without retaining the reins of constant responsibility is surely a clear clue as to the broadcaster's intention. It is to make as much money as possible.

Proprietors of the older media of mass communications, the more sober business men and thinkers in the field of journalism, long ago consigned to the ash-heap the advertising throw-away. The editors and the publishers get out their paper without the help, advice, or direction of the advertisers, and even edit the advertising copy on occasion. It is traditional that the good magazines and the good newspapers, those that have survived the test of readership decade after decade, abhor even the vaguest suggestion concerning news content or feature make-up from advertisers and their agents.

Radio can rearrange its position, even at this late date, if the broadcasters care to make the effort. Nothing is ever static, although at the time of a projected change the policy of precedent seems as unalterable as scientific law. The networks and the stations—in concert, or even singly—can take back from the advertisers the duties and privileges of broadcasting. They can decide, in the light of their broader experience, demagnetized of allegiance to a particular brand of soap, what the public interest and necessity really is, and they can become experts in radio instead of advertising specialists, relegating the sale of products to the same importance that it has in journalism—the back of the book.

And then, when the people of the United States rather than the board of directors of a patent medicine company are recognized as the true audience, radio can, perhaps, take its rightful place as a private enterprise, with whom the regulatory commissions have protective and constructive, rather than merely punitive, relationships.

RESPONDING TO THE PEOPLE'S WILL [4]

[Albert N.] Williams [see selection above] has strongly implied that advertisers consciously seek to destroy whatever of public interest might be offered American listeners.

This is specious and unworthy reasoning. It implies dishonor on the part of American manufacturers and, in effect, finds them guilty of some kind of oppressive collusion designed to undermine the public weal. I find it difficult to conjure visions of Procter and Gamble executives, as an example, surveying the mass impact of radio and concluding: "This is it, boys. We will take over the medium of radio and destroy public interest. There will be a by-product value to us as well. We'll sell some soap."

Mr. Williams continues, "Everybody knows the intent of a manufacturer. It is to sell as much of his product as he can." Few will quarrel with that proposition. Does he not, in selling as much of his produce as he can, serve the public interest? I realize, of course, that those who coined the chain-reaction phrase, "in the public interest, convenience and necessity," have not been called upon to define it. They are like the artisans

[4] From a letter by A. D. Willard, Jr., former Executive Vice President, National Association of Radio and Television Broadcasters, quoted in *Listening*, by Albert N. Williams. University of Denver Press. Denver. 1948. p78-82. Reprinted by permission.

who make parachutes: somebody else leaps from the plane, at considerable risk, to test them. But if we are to consider the public interest, must we not weigh all the factors of social practice: fair and full employment, freedom to work in freedom, liberty to seek after one's aspirations? Are not all of these democratic principles woven into the cloth of public interest? And if such is true, is not that vague but significant interest served in our economy by the free movement of goods? For in commerce, there is prosperity. And advertising serves well the cause of commerce.

So I refute the implication that advertisers bear witness against their brethren when they employ radio or any other medium of their choice.

I view with wonder Mr. Williams' conclusion that "it (radio) is operated in the specific interest of a handful of patent medicine makers, soap chemists and tobacco curers." Certainly, upon reflection, you must recognize this as a frivolous assertion. . . .

In truth there are well over a thousand broadcasting stations in the United States (and another couple of thousand on the way). They present programs supported by the advertising of literally tens of thousands of local and regional national advertisers, as diversified in interests and philosophies as any selected group of Americans might be. The fiction . . . that radio is "controlled" or, for that matter, even principally supported by a handful of advertisers usually refers to about fifteen or twenty large manufacturers—and in sum they represent something less than 20 per cent of radio's annual gross income. Indeed, the network programs of all the advertisers on all of our national networks account for less than 25 per cent of the income of America's radio stations.

No less curious is Mr. Williams' statement that "radio is not, today, any of the things it was born to be." Of course, I can only assume what the Williams' definition of the things it was born to be might be. But, by my definition (and the millions of listeners view it as an acceptable one) radio was born to be a medium of mass communication: it was born to perform in the interest of the greatest number. That the least among us should measure its worth entirely by its shortcomings, lends little support to our democratic principles of majority rule. I challenge the flat pronouncement that "radio is not operated in the public interest." Ample evidence to the contrary can be found in radio's truly astounding contribution to the war effort in mobilizing manpower and material, in selling bonds, in its unceasing and unstinted service to every facet of America's war effort . . . and the countless civic efforts to which it freely donates its time on community levels. Here again, the people of America agree—82 per cent of them consider radio's over-all service in their communities as "excellent" or "good"; indeed, better than the newspapers, the schools, the local government, or the churches. . . .

The broadcaster must have listeners in order to make money. This is no chicken and egg allegory. We know which comes first. To obtain an audience, he must program his station in a manner which attracts the attention and the affection of listeners: and he must be a man of sufficient good taste that he does not repel the public by tactics which operate against that public's interest.

Does it seem demonstrable to you that a broadcaster would risk a career and important capital on a venture in which he was determined to destroy his entity by bad manners and poor judgment? . . .

From a whisper, in less than three decades, . . . [radio] has become a mighty voice, participating in and influencing the lives of millions. I believe that that influence has been and is for the good of the many, though I will not deny its annoyance to the few. As to the popular observation in certain quarters that the air waves belong to the people, I must ask this: to whom do they belong in Russia?—in England? Perhaps by this time Mr. Williams has seen the dispatch from London (New York Times, January 24, 1947) reciting the complaint . . . that the British Broadcasting Corporation (a state-operated system) was showing preference to the left-wing speakers. It would appear, if the charges are substantiated, that in many parts of the world, the air waves, do, indeed, belong to the people—the people who are in power.

For my part, I would rather entrust the stewardship of these air waves to the thousand radio stations and the sixty thousand people who are employed by them in America's free radio system. They, and only they, are responsive to the will of a hundred million listeners who vote for or against their programs every day and to whom they (the broadcasters) and, yes, even their advertisers, must look each quarter hour of every day for listening and for support.

NEEDED: AN "ARM'S LENGTH" RELATIONSHIP [5]

The broadcasters need to achieve, immediately, that degree of arm's length relationship with the advertisers which fairly characterizes all but a submarginal handful of newspapers and magazines. . . .

It has been said that advertisers dictate policy in the print media, also. The studies of the Commission on Freedom of the Press indicate that the Commission does not believe this to be the fact in the vast majority of instances. Certain facts, however, seem too obvious to permit of debate. One is that the advertisers do not actually prepare the reading matter in the print media or weave their sales messages into the reading matter. Another is that the bulk of newspaper and magazine publishers do not regard the sale of goods and services as their only, or even their primary, reason for being.

It has been said that it makes no difference whether A, who writes radio shows, B, who produces them, C, who directs them, and D, E, and F, who act them, are on the pay roll of a broadcasting station or on the pay roll of an advertising agency. They would be bound to write, produce, direct, and act in precisely the same way. To say this is, it seems to the author, to miss completely the point made above.

It is hard to rationalize the statement. One invariably asks himself: Are they ignorant of the basic human desire to please

[5] From *The American Radio*, a special report of the Commission on Freedom of the Press, by Llewelyn White, Assistant Director of the Commission's staff. University of Chicago Press. Chicago. 1947. p225-7. Reprinted by permission.

whatever bosses man has, or is this a tacit admission that the broadcasters' goals are, in fact, the same as the advertisers': to sell goods and services?   It is like saying that . . . Ben Hibbs and Virginius Dabney would be just as satisfactory editors for . . . the *Saturday Evening Post* and the Richmond (Va.) *Times-Dispatch*, respectively, if they were employed by a national advertising agency.   It discounts, perhaps through ignorance, the classic "war" between editorial people and the "front office."   Indeed, it skims over the constant struggle between the creative people in radio, both those who work for the broadcasters and those who work for the advertisers, pay-roll-wise, and their masters—the advertiser and the advertiser-cowed broadcaster. . . .

It has been said that if any attempt were made to exclude advertising men from the preparation of radio's "reading matter," the advertising men (including the sponsors) would simply abandon radio to economic starvation.   Here we are asked to believe either that radio is not really so effective as an advertising medium as the broadcasters have been telling us and that the sponsors who have been using it were prompted solely by charitable motives or that their advertising messages could not stand on their own merits, as they are obliged to do in the other media, but must be slipped over on a public which otherwise would reject them; or that people do not listen to the commercials at the beginning and end of programs but only to middle commercials.

It is difficult . . . to reconcile these things with the broadcasters' repeated claims that radio is far and away the most effective medium for the advertisement of certain types of goods and services, that listeners actually "like" the commercials, and that the majority of them do not turn their sets off or down during the commercials between programs, even when these commercials are what are known as "local station-break spots" and are therefore wholly unrelated to the programs preceding and following them.

WHO PROMOTES "HARMFUL" TV? [6]

Like all Gaul, TV in the United States is divided into three chief parts—the sponsor, the advertising agent, and the station owner.

The sponsor pays the station owner for his time and other facilities. The advertising agent acts as middleman between the sponsor and the station owner, for which the sponsor pays him a commission. The man who pays, you will observe, is the sponsor; and you and I, the public, pay the sponsor by buying his goods or services. The important relationship, then, is the one between the sponsor and the public.

If you were to ask a hypothetical sponsor why he puts on certain presumably "harmful" [particularly to children] television programs, he might, first, brusquely ask by whose authority the programs are judged "harmful." You would, then, have to admit that the social sciences have no empirical data to support such an accusation. The best you could do would be to point out that many experts, after much scholarly observation, have charged that many TV programs are harmful. But you would have to admit that, from an objective standpoint, the experts so far have proved nothing. . . .

If the sponsor were candid he might drop his challenging attitude and take you, with confidence, into the heart of his dilemma. He would point out that TV, like the newspapers, the magazines, or the radio, is simply another medium which he uses to advertise his products; and that, in accord with prevailing custom and practice in business, he cannot justify spending a dollar in advertising unless it will bring more dollars in sales.

Continuing his confidential explanation, our sponsor would probably go on to say that he, personally, would like nothing better than to be able to put on television programs which everyone would find wholesome and unobjectionable. But his prime

⁶ From *Television and Our Children*, by Robert Lewis Shayon, radio and television critic, *Saturday Review* and *Christian Science Monitor*. Longmans, Green and Company. New York. 1951. p52-9. Reprinted by permission.

goal is, still, to maintain and increase sales. In order to do this, at justifiable cost, via TV, he must attract large audiences.

His advertising agent, who specializes in such matters, tells him that the only way to attract large audiences is to put on programs that attract the public. The programs that attract the public, according to the advertising agent, are, more often than not, the very ones which the critics consider either positively harmful, or, at the very least, negatively unsatisfactory.

How, asks the sponsor, is he to escape from his dilemma?

To put on most so-called "good" programs is to risk public inattention, and loss of sales. To lose sales is to suffer the disapproval of, and possible penalties from, his corporation and its stockholders. On the other hand, with no scientific evidence that the "bad" programs are really detrimental; with the public, so his advertising agent tells him, pleased with them; and with his sales curves, as a result, showing marked—in some cases remarkable—rises, what choice has he but to continue as he is doing at present? . . .

Your next step would be to have an equally frank talk with the sponsor's advertising agent. "On what basis," you might ask him, "do you advise your client that the programs which critics consider unsatisfactory and harmful are the very ones that attract the public?"

The advertising agent would reply that his recommendations are based on the vast amount of data accumulated by all known methods that measure the preference of audiences. These methods include telephone calls to, and personal interviews with, TV listeners, automatic devices that record the stations to which a set is tuned, and the keeping of listener diaries.

The agent would admit that all these methods have their limitations, but he would insist that they have always indicated that the majority of listeners generally prefer the kind of programs which are being put on, rather than the kind that TV critics are always badgering the sponsor to produce. By and large, the advertising agent would assert, the figures prove that the people like what they are getting on TV. . . .

You would then ask the agent how people can be expected to like what they do not get. You would declare that the record shows that the so-called "desirable" programs are, with certain rare exceptions, never put on at times when the largest audiences are available to see them, that is, during the early evening hours; and that when a "good" program is put on at a favorable period, it is hardly ever there long enough to give the listeners an opportunity to grow to like it. Here, the advertising agent might . . . ask [what] is the alternative? Deliberately to advise a client that he experiment with an untried program formula, and thus fly in the face of every trade shibboleth, would be to risk a fearsome drop in the sponsor's sales curve.

The advertising business is highly competitive, the agent would declare, and clients are known to be notoriously fickle, sometimes changing agencies with the proverbial speed of the pea in the shell game. . . .

You might then go to the station owner who carries the programs the advertising agent recommends to the sponsor. "I have been told," you might say, "that TV station owners are licensed by the government to operate in the public interest. I can understand, perhaps, how circumstances tend to compel the sponsor and the advertising agent to perpetuate the unsatisfactory program situation. But I do not understand why you, the station owner, vested as you are with the responsibility of protecting the public's interest, do not take immediate steps to remedy the situation."

The station owner . . . would tell you that late in 1945, and again in 1947, the National Association of Broadcasters financed a nation-wide investigation of the public's attitude toward radio. When the investigation was completed, the NAB hired Dr. Paul F. Lazarsfeld, the head of Columbia University's Bureau of Applied Social Research, to analyze the findings. Since radio's pattern is, obviously, being extended to television, the station owner would suggest that there is no reason why Dr. Lazarsfeld's conclusions cannot be applied with equal validity to TV. He would then read you what Dr. Lazarsfeld said, after reviewing the conventional arguments for and against "serious" and "educational" broadcasting:

"Few people want to learn by way of radio, but most critics agree that they should. Therefore the best thing for the broadcaster to do is to keep the volume of educational broadcasts slightly above what the masses want. In this way, he may contribute to a systematic rise in the general cultural level without defeating the educational goal by driving the audience away. This policy will disappoint some educators, and bore some listeners, but it is precisely the kind of compromise which must be found."

This is Dr. Lazarsfeld's conclusion. After reading it to you, our hypothetical station owner might, if he were quite candid, state flatly that the proposed Lazarsfeld compromise is simply out of the question. A station's chief revenue, he would remind you, comes from the sponsor. It is the sponsor who decides what is put on.

The station owner might, obligingly, tell you that there are proposals on record for solving the problem by the station itself, and the limiting of the sponsor to the advertising message; the dictating to the sponsor of what kind of programs he may produce; and the arbitrary setting aside of specific periods of time for station-produced programs with no advertising at all.

All these solutions, the station owner would assert, are unworkable. Unless an owner were eager to commit financial suicide, he could not possibly attempt to effect any such measures singlehanded. Universal agreement by all station owners to do the same would be necessary. It is a matter of record that station owners have never been able to agree on anything more meaningful than a harmless decency code.

Besides, each of the proposed solutions would mean either direct expense to the station owner or loss of revenue from the sponsor. The average station owner can afford neither of these choices, particularly at this crucial moment in TV's development, when all his assets are being plowed back into a fierce, competitive struggle for a place in television's future. The future is expected to be highly profitable but, at present, is enormously expensive.

When the station owner had finished, you might ask if he could suggest any way at all out of the dilemma. "Yes," he might say, "let the public make its wishes known to the sponsors." But if you protested that letter-writing campaigns and organized pressure groups face too many obvious obstacles, and that, consequently, they have failed, in the past, to have any significant results, our station owner would probably shake his head, and reply: "I cannot deny it. But this is a democracy. The machinery is there, but the people do not use it as fully as they should." . . .

The sponsor, the advertising agent, and the station owner have compelling reasons for putting on the kind of television programs that we see and hear. In order to challenge the pattern, they would have to accept serious financial risk. The more thoughtful among TV executives know full well that the social consequences of their actions may not be wholly desirable— even for their own children. Yet they continue to perpetuate the unhappy cycle of cause and effect.

This ethical duality, of course, is not unique to the television business. It cuts across the whole range of our way of life. It is that old problem of our double standard of socio-economic morality.

THE "CAPTIVE" AUDIENCE—I [7]

As soon as you pay your fare to ride on a bus or streetcar in Washington, D.C., St. Louis, Cincinnati or . . . [a score of] other cities, you discover that you are no longer a free American citizen. Automatically and involuntarily you have become a member of a "captive audience." Willy-nilly you must listen to raucous radio advertising.

In these . . . cities some four million regular passengers on public transit vehicles are being sold out to radio advertisers. Regardless of their rights, wishes or personal need for privacy, they are delivered like cattle on the hoof, at $1 per thousand head.

I have ridden Washington's captive buses in which tens of thousands of citizens must sit helplessly listening to batteries of loudspeakers (eight to a bus) placed two feet above their heads. Commercial programs blare from morning to night

[7] From "Must We All Join the Captive Audience?" by Holman Harvey, writer. *Reader's Digest.* 59:20-4. July 1951. Reprinted by permission.

without letup.   And to make certain that no messages miss their sitting targets, the loudspeakers have been installed without either cut-off or modulating switches.

As the noise of the motor increases within the bus, the broadcast volume automatically soars to surmount it.   The promoters, Transit Radio, Inc., of Cincinnati (TRINC), are especially proud of this "ambient noise control."   They are also delighted with their ingenious "beep circuit" which steps up the volume of the advertising announcements by 25 per cent. These two devices enable TRINC to assure its advertisers that passengers can't escape their messages: "If they can hear, they can hear your commercial!"   To make this slogan airtight, bus and streetcar drivers are under orders not to interfere with the broadcasting, whatever pleas may come from passengers.   Only in case of accident or mechanical difficulty may the sound be cut off!

The idea of exploiting bus and streetcar passengers as a captive audience for radio advertising barked its way onto the American scene in Cincinnati . . . [in 1948] There, for the first time in a century of take-it-or-leave-it advertising, TRINC could sell advertisers an audience that could be exactly counted (by paid fares) and that had no possible means of escape. TRINC calmly announced to the advertising world that it could "deliver" 600,000 Cincinnati passengers—at a dollar per thousand.   And deliver them it did.

Since then, armed with an apparently unbeatable formula, Transit Radio has raced from city to city across the nation. . . .

It is estimated that 82 per cent of the people who live in our cities use public vehicles and the average ride is 25 minutes. That is 50 minutes a day for the round trip.   This is almost an hour a day that thousands of students count upon for study, and millions of other folk use for reading or for quiet relaxation. It is their time, but it no longer is theirs to use as they wish. It has been stolen from them and sold for commercial profit.

The audience may be captive, but it is not taking the treatment sitting down.   TRINC has aroused bitter resentment among large numbers of passengers. Within a few months of its Washington debut, and although only a few of the city's 1500 buses and trolleys had been equipped, rebellion broke out. Backed by leading lawyers serving without fee, citizens stormed hearings held by the Public Utilities Commission and protested against the "rolling juke boxes." . . .

A typical hour's broadcast which emanates from a local FM radio station includes the news (given four times), the time, the weather, music and twelve "spot" advertising plugs—or one every five minutes.

TRINC is frank to say that its business is in its infancy and that it counts on complete radio control of the transportation facilities of the nation. It claims astonishing sales results already. Impressed by TRINC's slogan, "Mr. and Mrs. Everybody Ride the Buses and Streetcars," more than eighty national and regional advertisers have bought broadcast time.

On the local scene, in the . . . cities where is already has a captive audience, TRINC's foremost claim is that it can "deliver" women shoppers. Its promotion literature says: "They are the perfect advertising prospect, wide open to the power of suggestion. They alight from buses in a matter of minutes after hearing the TR (Transit Radio) commercial. No long memory carry-over is necessary. . . . TR hits them right on the nose."

Hundreds of retail stores—notably department stores, home furnishers and clothiers—are buying TRINC time to hit women on the nose. In one recent month, more than 400 retailers were buscasting at one time.

In Washington, however, rebellious riders have begun a struggle to end buscasting in the national capital and, if possible, to block its spread to other cities. The National Citizens Committee Against Forced Listening is keeping up a barrage of anti-TRINC publicity, while the Transit Riders Association has concentrated on a legal struggle which [has been carried] to the United States Supreme Court.[8] . . . Its case is based on the charge that buscasting infringes on passengers' liberties under the Bill of Rights.

It also insists that the question of how many passengers object is without bearing—that even a majority may not deprive other citizens of their basic liberties under law.

[8] See following selection.—Ed.

The vigilant American Civil Liberties Union has joined in the battle to support this contention. It declares: "There is developing a nation-wide pattern of forced listening thrust upon captive audiences. A legal validation of forced listening would set up a framework for future extension of this totalitarian method of capturing the minds of men."

THE "CAPTIVE" AUDIENCE—II [9]

(Mr. Justice Burton delivered the opinion of the Court.)

The principal question here is whether, in the District of Columbia, the Constitution of the United States precludes a street railway company from receiving and amplifying radio programs through loudspeakers in its passenger vehicles under the circumstances of this case. The service and equipment of the company are subject to regulation by the Public Utilities Commission of the District of Columbia. The Commission, after an investigation and public hearings disclosing substantial grounds for doing so, has concluded that the radio service is not inconsistent with public convenience, comfort and safety and "tends to improve the conditions under which the public ride." The Commission, accordingly, has permitted the radio service to continue despite vigorous protests from some passengers that to do so violates their constitutional rights. For the reasons hereafter stated, we hold that neither the operation of the service nor the action of the Commission permitting its operation is precluded by the Constitution.

The Capital Transit Company, here called Capital Transit, is a privately owned public utility corporation, owning an extensive street railway and bus system which it operates in the District of Columbia under a franchise from Congress. Washington Transit Radio, Inc., here called Radio, also is a privately owned corporation doing business in the District of Columbia. . . .

[9] From *Official Reports of Supreme Court,* v343, U.S. no3—v344, U.S., no2 [Cases adjudged in Supreme Court at October term 1951 and 1952 (opinions May 5—December 22, 1952)]. Superintendent of Documents. Washington 25, D.C. In this case, the Supreme Court of the United States reversed the decision of the Court of Appeals and upheld the right of public transportation companies to permit the use of commercially sponsored radio broadcasts in their vehicles. The outcry by some citizens (see article by Holman Harvey, above) has not stopped the spread of such broadcasting to a number of major cities.—Ed.

In March 1948, Capital Transit experimented with "music as you ride" radio programs received and amplified through loud speakers in a streetcar and in a bus. These vehicles were operated on various lines at various hours. A poll of passengers who heard the programs showed that 92 per cent favored their continuance. Experience in other cities was studied. Capital Transit granted Radio the exclusive right to install, maintain, repair and use radio reception equipment in Capital Transit's streetcars, buses, terminal facilities, waiting rooms and division headquarters. Radio, in return, agreed to contract with the broadcasting station for programs to be received during a minimum of eight hours every day, except Sundays. To that end Radio secured the services of station WWDC-FM. Its programs were to meet the specifications stated in Capital Transit's contract. Radio agreed to pay Capital Transit after a 90-day trial, $6 per month per radio installation, plus additional compensation dependent upon the station's receipts from sources such as commercial advertising on the programs. In February 1949, when more than twenty installations had been made, the service went into regular operation. At the time of the Commission's hearings, October 27-November 1, 1949, there were 212. On that basis the minimum annual payment to Capital Transit came to $15,264. The potential minimum would be $108,000, based upon 1500 installations. The contract covered five years, with an automatic five-year renewal in the absence of notice to the contrary from either party. . . .

[Franklin S.] Pollak and [Guy] Martin [complainants in the case] contend that the radio programs interfere with their freedom of conversation and that of other passengers by making it necessary for them to compete against the programs in order to be heard. The Commission, however, did not find, and the testimony does not compel a finding, that the programs interfered substantially with the conversation of passengers or with rights of communication constitutionally protected in public places. It is suggested also that the First Amendment guarantees a freedom to listen only to such points of view as the listener wishes to hear. There is no substantial claim that the programs have been used for objectionable propaganda. There is no issue of that kind before us. The inclusion in the program of a few announcements explanatory and commendatory of Capital Transit's own services does not sustain such an objection.

The court below [United States Court of Appeals, which upheld Pollak and Martin's view in its relation to "commercials"] has emphasized the claim that the radio programs are an invasion of constitutional rights of privacy of the passengers. This claim is that no matter how much Capital Transit may wish to use radio in its vehicles as part of its service to its passengers and as a source of income, no matter how much the great majority of its passengers may desire radio in those vehicles, and however positively the Commission, on substantial evidence, may conclude that such use of radio does not interfere with the convenience, comfort and safety of the service but tends to improve it, yet if one passenger objects to the programs as an invasion of his constitutional right of privacy, the use of radio on the vehicles must be discontinued. This position wrongly assumes that the Fifth Amendment secures to each passenger on a public vehicle regulated by the Federal Government a right of privacy substantially equal to the privacy to which he is entitled in his own home. However complete his right of privacy may be at home, it is substantially limited by the rights of others when its possessor travels on a public thoroughfare or rides in a public conveyance. Streetcars and buses are subject to the immediate control of their owner and operator and, by virtue of their dedication to public service, they are for the common use of all of their passengers. The Federal Government in its regulation of them is not only entitled, but is required, to take into consideration the interests of all concerned.

In a public vehicle there are mutual limitations upon the conduct of everyone, including the vehicle owner. These conflicting demands limit policies on such matters as operating schedules and the location of car or bus stops, as well as policies relating to the desirability or nature of radio programs in the vehicles. Legislation prohibiting the making of artificially amplified raucous sounds in public places has been upheld. . . .

Conversely, where a regulatory body has jurisdiction, it will be sustained in its protection of activities in public places when those activities do not interfere with the general public convenience, comfort and safety. The supervision of such practices by a Public Utilities Commission in the manner prescribed in the District of Columbia meets the requirements both of substantive and procedural due process when it is not arbitrarily and capriciously exercised.

The contention of Pollak and Martin would permit an objector, with a status no different from that of other passengers, to override not only the preference of the majority of the passengers but also the considered judgment of the federally authorized Public Utilities Commission, after notice, investigation and public hearings, and upon a record reasonably justifying its conclusion that the policy of the owner and operator did not interfere with public convenience, comfort and safety but tended, in general, to improve the utility service.

We do not agree with that contention. The protection afforded to the liberty of the individual by the Fifth Amendment against the action of the Federal Government does not go that far. The liberty of each individual in a public vehicle or public place is subject to reasonable limitations in relation to the rights of others.

This Court expresses no opinion as to the desirability of radio programs in public vehicles. In this case that is a matter for decision between Capital Transit, the public and the Public Utilities Commission. The situation is not unlike that which arises when a utility makes a change in its running schedules or in the locations of its stops in the interests of the majority of the passengers but against the vigorous protests of the few who are inconvenienced by the change.

While the court below expressly refrained from stating its view of the constitutionality of the receipt and amplification in public vehicles of musical programs containing no commercial advertising and other announcements, it is clear that if programs containing commercial advertising and other announcements are permissible, then programs limited to the type of music here contracted for would not be less so.

The judgment of the Court of Appeals, accordingly, is reversed and the case is remanded to the District Court. . . .

[Thus, the Supreme Court ruled, by a vote of seven to one, that the broadcast of commercial radio programs, and presumably television programs, to public vehicles, is constitutional. Mr. Justice Frankfurter took no part in the proceedings because, he said, "My feelings are so strongly engaged as a victim of the practice in controversy that I had better not participate in judicial comment upon it." Mr. Justice Douglas dissented, as follows.— Ed.]

This is a case of first impression. There are no precedents to construe; no principles previously expounded to apply. We write on a clean slate.

The case comes down to the meaning of "liberty" as used in the Fifth Amendment. Liberty in the constitutional sense must mean more than freedom from unlawful governmental restraint; it must include privacy as well, if it is to be a repository of freedom. The right to be let alone is indeed the beginning of all freedom. Part of our claim to privacy is in the prohibition of the Fourth Amendment against unreasonable searches and seizures. It gives the guarantee that a man's home is his castle beyond invasion either by inquisitive or by officious people. A man loses that privacy of course when he goes upon the streets or enters public places. But even in his activities outside the home he has immunities from controls bearing on privacy. He may not be compelled against his will to attend a religious service; he may not be forced to make an affirmation or observe a ritual that violates his scruples; he may not be made to accept one religious, political, or philosophical creed as against another. Freedom of religion and freedom of speech guaranteed by the First Amendment give more than the privilege to worship, to write, to speak as one chooses; they give freedom not to do nor to act as the government chooses. The First Amendment in its respect for the conscience of the individual honors the sanctity of thought and belief. To think as one chooses, to believe what one wishes are important aspects of the constitutional right to be let alone.

If we remembered this lesson taught by the First Amendment, I do not believe we would construe "liberty" within the meaning of the Fifth Amendment as narrowly as the Court does. The present case involves a form of coercion to make people listen. The listeners are of course in a public place; they are on streetcars traveling to and from home. In one sense it can be said that those who ride the streetcars do so voluntarily. Yet in a practical sense they are forced to ride, since this mode of transportation is today essential for many thousands. Compulsion which comes from circumstances can be as real as compulsion which comes from a command.

The streetcar audience is a captive audience. It is there as a matter of necessity, not of choice. One who is in a public vehicle may not of course complain of the noise of the crowd and the babble of tongues. One who enters any public place sacrifices some of his privacy. My protest is against the invasion of his privacy over and beyond the risks of travel.

The government may use the radio (or television) on public vehicles for many purposes. Today it may use it for a cultural end. Tomorrow it may use it for political purposes. So far as the right of privacy is concerned the purpose makes no difference. The music selected by one bureaucrat may be as offensive to some as it is soothing to others. The news commentator chosen to report on the events of the day may give overtones to the news that please the bureau head but which rile the streetcar captive audience. The political philosophy which one radio speaker exudes may be thought by the official who makes up the streetcar programs to be best for the welfare of the people. But the man who listens to it on his way to work in the morning and on his way home at night may think it marks the destruction of the Republic.

One who tunes in on an offensive program at home can turn it off or tune in another station, as he wishes. One who hears disquieting or unpleasant programs in public places, such as restaurants, can get up and leave. But the man on the streetcar has no choice but to sit and listen, or perhaps to sit and to try *not* to listen.

When we force people to listen to another's ideas, we give the propagandist a powerful weapon. Today it is a business enterprise working out a radio program under the auspices of government. Tomorrow it may be a dominant political or religious group. Today the purpose is benign; there is no invidious cast to the programs. But the vice is inherent in the system. Once privacy is invaded, privacy is gone. Once a man is forced to submit to one type of radio program, he can be forced to submit to another. It may be but a short step from a cultural program to a political program.

If liberty is to flourish, government should never be allowed to force people to listen to any radio program. The right of privacy should include the right to pick and choose from competing entertainments, competing propaganda, competing political philosophies. If people are let alone in those choices, the right of privacy will pay dividends in character and integrity. The strength of our system is in the dignity, the resourcefulness, and the independence of our people. Our confidence is in their ability as individuals to make the wisest choice. That system cannot flourish if regimentation takes hold. The right of privacy, today violated, is a powerful deterrent to any one who would control men's minds.

BROADCASTING AS A MEDIUM OF EDUCATION

EDITOR'S INTRODUCTION

Broadcasting is universally recognized as an instrument of entertainment and general information. But it has made progress much more slowly as a medium of education. As Mrs. Greenwood indicates in the final article of this section, radio broadcasting has never been used to its fullest advantage for adult education, and radio is only of minor assistance in elementary and high school classrooms.

What about educational television? Educators throughout the nation are aware of the challenge to accept the opportunities offered by television or perhaps to let the chance go for all time. There are some educators who do not regard the challenge seriously, feeling that the usefulness of TV would be severely limited in the classroom, even if the always present problem of finances were solved.

The recent developments in New York State, as discussed in two articles herein, do not augur well for the rapid expansion of educational television. But it is too soon for the TV enthusiasts among educators to despair. The example of the use of television for instruction at home, as related by Mr. Barden, indicates what can be done.

NEW HORIZONS FOR EDUCATORS [1]

[Early in 1952] the Federal Communications Commission authorized an improved and expanded system of national television which increased the number of channels from twelve to eighty-two and which will make possible upwards of 2000 stations in 1300 communities. These stations can cover a radius of

[1] From an address by Paul A. Walker, Chairman, Federal Communications Commission, delivered at the Annual Education Congress, Harrisburg, Pa., October 2, 1952. Mimeographed text available from the Commission. Washington, D.C. 1952. Reprinted by permission.

from forty to seventy miles or more, and they can operate around the clock. Moreover, the allocation table is so arranged that there can be a fair distribution of these stations over the entire nation, calculated to serve the small towns and rural areas as well as the big cities.

To appreciate the scope of this new system, we can compare it with our radio system which has 2350 stations on the air—but after thirty years of broadcasting, many of these radio stations can operate only in the daytime. And many of those operating at night can be heard satisfactorily for only a few miles.

More American communities can have a television station of their own than now have a daily newspaper of their own. There is no doubt that this marvelous technological development to flash sound and images over an entire nation at the speed of light is destined to become our dominant medium of mass communications. Now, what are the implications of this for education?

We know some highly provocative facts already. For example, we know that many children in television homes spend as much time before the television set as they do in school. We observe the rapt attention given to television by millions of adults. So, television is already in the business of education, educating both children and adults in its own special fashion.

But what about educators in television? . . . Educators could not see their way clear to participate in this medium when the original allocation of twelve channels was made in 1945. But as television mushroomed after the war and they saw its unrivaled impact, they became concerned over their role in it.

Their opportunity for action came when the FCC ordered a freeze on further construction of new stations in the former system of twelve channels and held a hearing to determine, among other things, the feasibility of greatly enlarging the system by adding seventy channels in the ultra-high frequency band.

Individual schools and organizations under the banner of the national Joint Committee on Educational Television petitioned the FCC to reserve channels for noncommercial educational use. In the latter part of 1950 and in the early part of 1951, the Joint Committee brought more than seventy witnesses—educators, national leaders, statesmen—from all parts of the nation to testify.

More than 800 colleges, universities, school systems and public service agencies filed formal statements supporting the request for a reservation of educational channels.

Among the many points that were made to the Commission were these:

Television is a tool comparable only to the invention of printing in its power to inform and to influence thought.

Educational television could raise the cultural and educational level of the masses of the American people to an unprecedented degree in a generation.

Television could revolutionize education—especially in the rural areas.

Television could bring the sense of actual operation of industry and the performance of governmental functions to the classroom.

That there was ample precedent for reserving channels for education in the action of the Federal Government making grants of land for the land grant colleges and universities.

That reliance on voluntary cooperation from commercial stations is not a substitute for the educators having their own stations.

On the basis of the entire record, the Commission . . . [on] April 14 [1952] took what has been called one of the most significant steps ever taken in this nation on behalf of education.

This came when the Commission issued its final report on its television allocation proceedings.

The Commission set aside for the exclusive use of American education 12 per cent of the total number of television channels assigned. This makes possible channel assignments for 242 noncommercial educational television stations. And even more may be added under certain conditions.

This reservation means that educators can now take their rightful place as educators via television.

The reservation means that in each of those 242 areas—[each] ranging over a radius of from forty to seventy miles or more— the educators now have an opportunity to employ this powerful tool of mass communications to serve the educational needs of that area as they feel they should be met.

The reservation makes possible the fullest and the freest experimentation and development by each community in the field of classroom instruction, out-of-classroom instruction and wholesome entertainment for the children and systematic courses as well as general informative and cultural programs for the adults by television.

The advent of this electronic tool occurs at a time when American educators are facing burdens of grave magnitude. A nation which has assumed a position of world leadership at a time of extreme international tension and at a time of galloping industrial and scientific progress is looking to its educators to prepare its children and its adult citizens alike for their new responsibilities.

American educators need all the help they can get in meeting their problems—including the help of television. The United States Office of Education tells us that 300,000 classrooms are needed immediately in our elementary and high schools. And, because of the increase in population, another 300,000 will be needed in 1958. We know that anything that television can do to assist the teachers—in which field there is a shortage of 53,000—will be welcome.

We know that one half of the American boys and girls qualified to attend college cannot enroll because of lack of funds. Although we have 1850 colleges and universities, there are not enough of them and they are not conveniently located.

Looking at the fourth level of education—adult education—we can see most serious inadequacies in our present methods and facilities. . . . We are confronted [for example] by the uncomfortable fact that in this rich and powerful nation we have ten million functional illiterates. They are handicapped in their home life, personal growth, citizenship, social activities, and, of course, in their occupational opportunities. Television could be employed to teach these illiterates in the privacy and comfort of their homes. Such instruction by television can help make them more able citizens, more valuable to industry, more valuable to the armed forces and better consumers.

WHO SHALL RUN EDUCATIONAL TV? [2]

Television can be a splendid teacher not only for school and college students, but also for great masses of adults who would like to gain now what they may have missed in their own school-days. . . .

But . . . television stations cost money—lots of it. Can the private colleges, already hard-pressed for cash, stand the added expense? And will the states and municipalities—with the exception of the wealthiest ones—be able to stretch their budgets to include educational TV?

On the other hand, there is danger that a golden opportunity for education will be lost by postponing action now. For unless considerable progress is shown [promptly] toward making effective use of the new channels, . . . the FCC may make . . . [the channels reserved for educational purposes] available to commercial applicants. [Only twenty-one applications for channels had been made by educational groups up to February 14, 1953.] Television's greatest recommendation as an educator lies in its ability to reach the great mass audience—to teach in a classroom with a million seats.

Educational TV can bring the light of learning into the rooms of shut-in children. Piped into high school and college classrooms, television can, by picture and word, heighten the interest in geography, history, literature, and a host of other subjects. Many more medical students can witness a piece of surgery when it is televised than when it is performed in the confines of an operating room.

These are the promises of TV. What are the hard facts?

Some educators say they are ready to sustain noncommercial stations, to raise money for their construction and program them on a day-to-day basis. Others approve the idea, but adopt the attitude of "Let George do it."

Behind it all is the silent but relentless drive of commercial expansion in the multimillion dollar industry TV has become in a

[2] From "Which Way for Educational TV?" by Harold Brown, formerly staff writer, New York *Herald Tribune. Senior Scholastic.* 61:5-6. October 29, 1952. Reprinted by permission of the editors of Scholastic Magazines.

few short years. The argument is heard that all channels should be turned over to commercial applicants. They have the money, the know-how, and they will set aside the hours for education. But they have not done so in the past.

The whole program has not been clearly defined. Who is to operate the stations? The states? The colleges backed by interested groups? Educators habitually move slowly toward their goals. Is there danger the dream may be lost? In short: Is educational television practical today? Here are some of the sides to a many-sided question.

Let the Colleges Do It

Educational television is the job of the colleges. With the help of civic-minded organizations they can build the stations and provide the best programs.

A number of colleges have already made a start in television. A few, like Johns Hopkins University in Baltimore, have passed beyond the experimental stage in their work in the new medium. The Johns Hopkins weekly "Science Review" program, produced in cooperation with the Du Mont Network, has already become part of the regular classroom work in many schools.

The University of California has been successfully broadcasting a credit course in child psychology. Applications for new channels have been granted to Kansas State College of Agriculture and Applied Science and the University of Houston, Texas, for a cooperative station with the public schools.[3]

Colleges have the research facilities, the great teachers, and the desire to present to the public the latest advances in health, agriculture, mental hygiene, marketing, nutrition, conservation, art, music, and civics.

It is the job of the colleges to teach, to provide education free of controls whether they be commercial or governmental. The colleges have the greatest stake in this great new medium of education. And they must accept their responsibilities toward educational TV.

[3] See also the following selection on Western Reserve University's program.—
Ed.

The cost will be large, of course. It is estimated that to build a new station will require anywhere from $150,000 to $750,000. It will cost another $100,000 for average annual operating costs. Most college heads, confronted with ever-rising costs, will shudder at these additional burdens.

But these figures do not mean the colleges can't do it. Help from outside organizations may be on the way. The Ford Foundation has made a $5 million grant to the Fund for Adult Education. The money will be used to search out practical methods of developing educational TV and, in some cases, to help finance educational stations.

But among the educators themselves there seems to be a feeling that although the theory is right some one else should do the work. A recent survey showed that 57 per cent of the educators questioned believed in educational TV stations. However, further investigation showed that many of these educators have no intentions of getting their colleges into television themselves.

Let the States Do It

It's time to get a move on, and if the colleges can't do the job, then the states must do it for them.

The whole opportunity may be lost through lack of positive action by the colleges. It is the opinion of many people that the states, through their departments of education, must apply for the channels. With the cost carried by the taxpayers, the states must build the stations.

There is nothing new, it is argued, about state interest in education. Indeed the states have the responsibility under the Constitution to provide free public education.

New York State, through its Board of Regents, has been the first to apply for the noncommercial channels made available by the FCC. It has applied for a ten-channel network, including one station in New York City. Permits for three of these have been granted.

The New York State Board of Regents does not at this time have the money or the legislative authority to go ahead with its proposed . . . TV network. However, Governor Thomas E.

Dewey has appointed a fifteen-member TV commission to work on the problem. . . .[4]

Connecticut and New Jersey are working on similar plans, but time is of the essence.

Having the state operate educational TV channels is fairer than having them operated by individual colleges or universities. In New York City only one channel has been allocated for about eight million people. Fordham University was interested in the station, but state operation will provide opportunities for all the city's colleges and schools to share in the channel.

Can the states provide the necessary programming? In New York State, the Regents have at their disposal the facilities of seven thousand public schools, two thousand private schools, 136 colleges, universities and institutes, and about a thousand libraries, historical societies and museums.

Nevertheless, objections to state operation have been raised. Of course, the New York plan contains safeguards to prevent the network from being used for propaganda purposes. But there is danger that sometime, somewhere, unscrupulous men could use these channels of communication to advance their own political ends.

Let the Broadcasters Do It

The FCC should revise its ruling and turn the educational channels back to commercial operators who have the funds and the know-how.

The FCC is not unanimous on the advisability of allocating noncommercial channels. It voted 3-2 . . . [in July 1952] in favor of granting the first four permits. The two members who dissented said the applicants had not shown financial qualifications. They pointed out that legislative action would be needed to provide the money.

Taxpayers are already smarting under the ever-increasing cost of education. Why face them with this new burden of owning television stations? There are many private corporations eager to put up the money for new stations, provided they have a fair chance of earning returns. Allocating the channels to these

[4] For a report of the Commission's decision see p 137-41.—Ed.

private corporations would be in keeping with our policy of free, competitive enterprise, a policy that has made America great.

This is the strongest argument for private operation of all channels. But there are others. The networks have had six years in which to develop TV techniques. They have become experts. There is no point in having an educational show if it is so badly done that no one will look at it.

The supporters of privately-operated TV admit that in the past the networks have paid nothing but lip-service to educational TV. But they claim that if the reserved channels are thrown open to them, arrangements can be made that would require them to devote a larger percentage of TV time to educational programs. Maybe they can make educational TV pay.

EDUCATIONAL TELEVISION IN
NEW YORK STATE—I [5]

A decision is now in the making in New York State which is destined to affect the education of our children for generations to come. This decision, which will have enormous implications for the adult population as well, is whether we shall have educational television in New York.

The challenge facing the people of this state is crucial but simple: Are our television channels, which are part of the public domain, with their unprecedented capacity for bringing vivid instruction to untold millions, to be utilized, at least in small part, for noncommercial educational purposes? Or should this most vital of our natural resources—affecting the very molding of our minds—be turned over in their entirety to commercial interests?

What exactly is educational TV? It is the operation of non-commercial television stations devoted to regularly scheduled courses of instruction for children and adults, in cities as well as in rural areas; the programs to be integrated with the state educational system and prepared by local television councils drawn from schools and cultural institutions in the area.

[5] From an article by Jacob L. Holtzmann, member of the New York State Board of Regents. New York *Times*. p X 13. January 11, 1953. Reprinted by permission.

At this time we foresee these broad lines of development: A major branch of the operation will be material transmitted directly to the classroom, to supplement school instruction. Imagine how our science classes would be enriched by presentation on TV of an elaborate experiment in plant growth or physiology! Consider the possibilities of illustrated lectures on music, direct from a rehearsal hall of the Philharmonic; of dramatized episodes bringing the American past vividly to life; of "live" journeys to famous museums.

Think of the opportunity for more than two million of our children sitting in their classroms in the thousands of schools across the state to see and hear the most important personalities of their day.

Also it will be possible through educational TV to take advantage of the special talents of individual educators, people with a particular gift in a certain field. Their genius will be made available from time to time to every classroom in the state; not as a substitute for personal instruction by the indispensable classroom teacher, but as a valuable adjunct.

The television programs will be carefully integrated into each of the courses in the curriculum of the future. Because of limitation of time and utility they will necessarily be restricted to no more than a program or two per day for any class. A predetermined schedule will fix the time for each of the programs and the subject matter to be taught. Homework and preliminary class work will be directed toward the program and the broadcast will provide a springboard for a vigorous discussion.

But the classroom is only part of the story. Education is a continuous process. It does not stop when youth finishes school or college—or where circumstances have forced a premature end to formal schooling. Adult education offers a rich field for educational TV.

Enrollment in New York State's adult education classes now totals half a million men and women. Another 50,000 are working for a high-school diploma in evening high schools, and additional tens of thousands are enrolled in college part-time courses, study clubs, farm and home bureau meetings.

For all of these culturally hungry people, educational TV can open infinite vistas. Courses in the areas of health, technology and the arts can be effectively presented—and at hours fixed solely for the convenience of the viewer. For women, such practical subjects as nutrition, child care, budgeting, dressmaking and household decoration can be brought into the home.

Under the plan of the Board of Regents, the state would furnish the funds for installing eleven stations—an estimated $350,000 for each, less than one third of the cost of a simple modern school building. It would also provide the necessary technical and administrative personnel, and such over-all services as networking facilities, kinescoping, and the organizing of film libraries.

The technical operating cost was estimated at $149,000 per station yearly. Actual programming would be left to a council administering each station, made up of cooperating representatives of the local institutions: high schools, colleges, libraries and museums.

But can we afford all this? Let's examine the figures. The $3.5 million installation cost for the entire educational TV system is no more than the approximate cost of constructing two miles of road in a state parkway. It is slightly less than 1 per cent of the current state budget for education, and an even more minute fraction of the billion dollars spent annually on education in New York by public and private bodies.

As for the expense of programming, the existing resources of the eight thousand educational and cultural institutions in this state, in materials and manpower, are more than adequate for handling the projected system. Under the state-wide network arrangement, if each of the ten participating cities contributed a single hour of programming per day, a full daily schedule of ten hours would be filled.

The question has been raised of possible abuse of its powers by a state-controlled network in the direction of political partisanship. These misgivings have no basis in fact. The educational TV network would not only be subject to the FCC safeguards but would operate under the close scrutiny of the Legislature.

Furthermore, the American school system has never violated the public trust to favor any political faction.

Finally, the question is asked: "Why not let commercial stations handle educational TV?" The answer is that those stations cannot afford the time to broadcast the volume of educational programs needed to serve the people of our state. They are in business to make money and rightly so. Their major source of income is through advertising, with the result that sponsored programs will always have high priority over any non-revenue-producing programs.

EDUCATIONAL TELEVISION IN NEW YORK STATE—II [6]

On April 14, 1952, the Federal Communications Commission announced the allocation of 242 television channels in the United States to be used exclusively for noncommercial, educational purposes. Ten ultra-high frequency channels were allocated to New York State, the allocation being valid until June 2, 1953.

As of . . . [February 1953] no state in the Union has, by legislative action, undertaken to utilize any of the channels allocated.

Pursuant to the provisions of Chapter 479 of the Laws of 1952 as amended, . . . [the] Temporary State Commission on the Use of Television for Educational Purposes is charged with responsibility of reporting on the use of television for educational purposes, including a proposal that the State of New York should build, own and operate a chain of ten ultra-high frequency television stations.

Under the proposal the state government would be expected to pay the cost of constructing and equipping this television network and also to pay the cost, in whole or in part, of maintaining and operating each of the stations with the necessary engineering, technical, programming and production staffs, as well

[6] From text of majority report, Temporary State Commission on the Use of Television for Educational Purposes, New York State. New York *Times*, p 16. February 25, 1953. Reprinted by permission. On February 24, 1953, this Commission voted, 10-5, to reject the proposal for a state-owned network of educational television stations as described by Jacob L. Holtzmann in the previous article in this section.—Ed.

as maintenance and administrative expenses and replacement of equipment. . . .

There is general agreement that television can be and has been used successfully for certain educational purposes.

In the field of adult education there have been extensive experiments with widely varying results both in the quality of the programs and in the size of the audiences they command.

Whether it is useful for academic teaching in the classroom remains to be established.

We are agreed that, with continued experimentation, the use of television for educational purposes may become increasingly valuable.

A sharp distinction must be drawn between the value of educational television and the manner in which it is operated and financed. Many educational programs are now being carried by commercial stations, with time and all technical, production and engineering costs paid by the stations. The free program time offered by commercial stations to the colleges, universities and public schools of the state has been only partially accepted.

The commission believes that the use of television for educational and cultural purposes is a desirable objective. There is no evidence before us that state-owned and operated stations are necessary or desirable for the achievement of this objective. . . .

Upon the basis of the actual costs of the smaller stations now operating throughout the country, the annual operating expense of a state-operated network would appear to be a minimum of $8.25 million. Since there has as yet been no experience with a noncommercial educational station, no figures are available to anticipate the details of operating expenses for such a station.

As a substitute for network and film productions on commercial stations, it is proposed that educational films be used. The cost of producing a thirty-minute educational film would range between $10,000 and $25,000, with an average of perhaps $20,000. If only one such film were to be produced each day, five days a week, for forty weeks in the year, the cost of film production alone would run to $4 million a year.

While it is assumed that educational films produced elsewhere would be available, there would be many hours when films produced by the state would be needed to fill out a program day.

If the major use of educational television is to be the show-ing of educational films, there has been no testimony before the commission that this could not be accomplished by the simple use of motion picture projectors and screens now available in most schools.

It is the conclusion of the commission that the evidence does not warrant the expenditure of large sums of public funds for state-owned and operated television stations.

The information before the commission indicates that the audience appeal of educational television programs on commer-cial stations to date has been small. Programs on commercial sta-tions which provide general information and coverage of public events have larger audiences. We do not assume educational sta-tions are intended for the purpose of duplicating the broadcast-ing of such events. . . .

Of equal importance with the questions as to the size of audi-ence for the proposed stations is the question whether educators will find it feasible to devote the time necessary to produce a con-tinuous flow of good programs. The commission has inquired extensively on this subject.

We find that the largest total number of hours which any group of educational institutions would provide is in the Buffalo area, amounting to 17.75 hours a week during an academic year of thirty-six to forty weeks.

In the Rochester area the educational institutions estimated that they could now provide ten to twelve hours, up to a possible maximum of fifteen hours a week.

Educational institutions in other areas were willing to promise only smaller amounts. We believe that far more than two or three hours a day would be necessary to justify venturing upon this immense enterprise of a chain of state-owned and operated television stations.

There is no satisfactory evidence before the commission that the commercial stations of the state will not continue to supply all the time for educational television which can be used. Com-mercial stations are required by the Federal Communications

Commission, as a condition of their license, to devote a certain amount of time to public service programs.

There is substantially no evidence before the commission that any educational institution has been deprived of time which it was prepared to fill with educational programs. On the contrary, all commercial stations have carried educational programs and a great many have offered free time on a regular basis to public schools, colleges and universities which have never taken full advantage of the offers. . . .

Programming in television is a highly skilled technique, laborious to learn and hard work to execute. Even though professional standards need not apply to educational programs, much detailed work and research is necessary to the success of any television production. To the extent that time is devoted to television productions it is apparent that an equal amount of time may be taken away from teaching duties or other existing responsibilities of the educators involved. . . .

As experimentation with educational television continues, it may be found that educators will be able to use more and more of the time which is now available to them on commercial stations and not yet accepted. In such cases, of course, readjustment of school staff schedules will be necessary.

The way to determine the amount of time education can use is by the process of intelligent development on a gradual basis. Any other course might prove to be a serious setback to the cause of education and of educational television. Progressive development of the use of existing facilities appears to us to be the sound approach.

Some advocates of a state-owned and operated system have said they would fill out the hours of the day by the use of current events material. The presentation of news and current events on commercial stations is now extensive. It is not the function of the state to duplicate these programs or to compete with private enterprise in this area any more than it is the function of the state to compete with private enterprise in the operation of radio stations, newspapers or other instruments of communications.

The commission is aware of the fact that all units of government are having difficulty balancing their budgets. There is also pressure for increasing spending by all units of government, which would mean the imposition of new taxes.

In the field of education there is continuous pressure for ever-increasing amounts of money, both from the localities and the state. It seems unwise to launch on a program of government operated television stations costing many millions of dollars when other inexpensive means of presenting all possible programs are available.

COLLEGE COURSES VIA TV [7]

The truth about cutting the Gordian knot, according to Plutarch, is that Alexander accomplished his purpose by unhitching the shaft of the chariot and leaving the knot alone.

The truth about the knotty problem of education by television appears to be that a good teacher putting his learning across is good television. Leaving the knotty problem alone, Western Reserve University simply hitched some good professors to a commercial television station for purposes of credit and noncredit instruction. It is the biggest classroom in the world.

In Cleveland today there are, according to a commercial survey made by Videodex, Inc., 27.5 thousand television sets tuned in five days a week, 9-9:30 A.M., to University Telecourses on Station WEWS, Channel 5, a commercial station. This is a 5.5 rating and places the telecourses close to the top ratings achieved by any televised presentations in the morning hours. Of the 813 students registered on a credit or noncredit basis, sixty-one credit students are doing the written work prescribed by telecourse syllabuses in Psychology 101 and forty two in Comparative Literature 239. Psychology 101 is the university's basic course in psychology. Comparative Literature 239 is concerned with modern European literature since 1914.

The written work of the 103 credit students is mailed in for criticism and grading by the faculty and is returned to the students by mail. Six to eight times more written work is required for a telecourse than for the same course given on campus. Tele-

[7] From "Instruction by Television and Home Study," by John P. Barden, Professor of Political Science, Western Reserve University. *School and Society.* 74: 374-6. December 15, 1951. Reprinted by permission.

course "classroom" time runs a little less than half that of the comparable campus course. Telecourse students . . . come to the campus for their final examinations. . . . The examinations will be the same as those taken by campus students. The credit granted upon successful completion of the telecourse will be applicable to any bachelor's degree offered for undergraduates by the university. Use of the credit, of course, depends upon due admission to degree candidacy in the university.

In addition to the 103 credit students, paying the regular fees for the telecourses, there are 710 noncredit students following the courses with syllabuses secured by registering with the university as noncredit students, and an average of five noncredit registrations a day continue to come in.

Besides the 813 registered students in the telecourses who reside in 101 cities and towns of northern Ohio and western Pennsylvania, many people have called or written to say that anywhere from three to ten neighbors are gathering in their homes each morning at 9 A.M. for the telecourses. After the session a discussion ensues on psychology or literature, as the case may be (Psychology 101—Mondays, Wednesdays, Fridays; Comparative Literature 239—Tuesdays, Thursdays). Several ladies have gloatingly told me that they are doing very well indeed without those old syllabuses costing $5. At a local veterans hospital the boys are taking the telecourses by the ward.

One lady notified us of another technique going the rounds. Two friends, each with television sets, listen to the telecourse presentations, then conduct a telephone discussion of the problems raised. The discussions take anywhere from fifteen minutes to an hour and a half. The telecourses have literally become the talk of the town's housewife population.

Local libraries report on unprecedented demand for the books on the telecourse lists. The telecourses are probably the first television performances that have succeeded in getting people to read books.

Received to date are 1520 letters running a gamut of compliment from faint praise to rave notice. More than three thousand requests for information have been filled.

IS TV THE ENEMY OF EDUCATION? [8]

Mary Adams leaned back in her study hall chair and yawned, stifling it as quickly as she could. Somehow, she just couldn't get down to her algebra homework. "Why, oh why," she thought to herself, "did I stay up to watch television? It wasn't that good . . . or was it?"

At the next table John Baker was pitching into the same algebra assignment with gusto. In Johnny's home there are a few strict family rules. One is: No television until homework is done, and no staying up past usual bedtime for TV. Johnny wanted to get part of his homework out of the way, so that he could see the night baseball game on TV.

Sitting across from John was Helen Carmodi. Helen saw a dramatization of *Vanity Fair* on television last week. She enjoyed it so much that she was now reading the novel.

Bob Downs was doing his history assignment, occasionally pausing to think about the afternoon's football practice. Bob's family doesn't have a television set. Although he sometimes watches programs in his friends' homes, TV has no real effect on his day-to-day activities.

Now if you asked Mary, and others like her, about the effect of television on her life, you'd get one kind of answer. If you asked John, Helen, or Bob, you would get three different replies. What's your opinion? Is television interfering with . . . school work? . . . To put it in other words, our question is: *Is television the enemy of education?*

Yes !

. . . Most high school boys and girls realize that there is work to be done. Given a fair break, they normally have their assignments ready when they reach school in the morning.

But many students aren't getting that "fair break." Television has already invaded . . . [many millions of] American

[8] From "TV—Enemy of Education?" by Herbert L. Marx, Jr., formerly Associate Editor, Scholastic Magazines. *Senior Scholastic*. 57:20-1. September 20, 1950. Reprinted by permission of the editors of Scholastic Magazines.

homes. With more than a hundred TV stations already in operation, the number of homes with television is mushrooming.

The plain fact is that television is getting in the way of more
important activities. Perhaps what is suffering most is homework.

Among Roselle, New Jersey, high school students who watch
TV regularly, grades dropped more than 15 per cent. In Stam-
ford, Connecticut, another survey showed that one third of the
students with TV sets find that television interferes with their
homework frequently or once in a while. The principal of a
Clifton, New Jersey, public school blamed television for the
sharp increase in failing grades among students. Similar surveys
in Chicago and New York City prove that TV is taking its toll
of school work.

In a few communities it has been proposed that students remain in school for extra hours each day—to make sure they get
their homework done without TV interference. TV—good or
bad—is cutting into studies.

And so much of television consists of poor, useless programs.
Of course, no one denies that television offers some fine entertainment, as well as some original educational programs. But
too few people bother to select the good programs (drama, news,
discussions, etc.) from the bad (old blood and thunder western
films you wouldn't dream of going to the movie theatre to see,
slapstick variety shows, and a generous number of just plain
boring programs.)

As one expert explains it, young TV audiences (and adults,
too!) "take what is put before them. A giant has come into the
homes of our nation which threatens to gobble up the normal
trend of family living. Television has become an electric nurse-
maid that dominates completely the lives of our children."

Most Americans suffer from a strange disease. It is called
"spectatoritis." Millions of Americans prefer watching baseball
to playing the game—or even to taking a walk. Among teen-
agers, however, spectatoritis has never had a very strong hold.
Young Americans are vigorous and enjoy all kinds of active
sports.

At least, this was true before television. Now thousands of
teen-agers spend leisure hours in the late afternoon and early
evening seated before television sets. They daily lose hours of
healthy athletic relaxation, as well as the rewards and excitement
of team play.

Not only sports are left behind as Captain Video takes over.
Evening "bull sessions" and "hen parties" are shushed into
silence as all eyes are glued to the TV screen. It may be true
that television keeps the family together more than in the "old
days" of movies and a spin in the car. But what is gained by
having Mom, Dad, and the kids sit together silently in a semi-
dark living room?

Leisure reading is a vital part of education. An evening with
a good book or magazine can provide entertainment, information,
and relaxation. Good reading habits, developed during school
days, carry over into adult life. By reading newspapers, magazines, and books, grown-ups continue their education all through
life. But the TV invasion has left its mark here, too. In Washington, D.C., adults with TV sets admitted to spending one
third less time reading books. In surveys among students much
the same results are found.

Reading, athletics, hobbies, and just chit-chat are all important in young people's education and character development.
And these things are gradually being wiped out by their common enemy, television. Until we learn to control the electronic
"giant" in our living room, television is the enemy of education
and the foe of family living.

No !

Television the enemy of education? Far from it! Television
is a great boon to education. Its possibilities have only begun to
be tapped.

In classrooms . . . [shortly after the Communist attack in
Korea there were plenty of lively discussions. When it came] to
discussing the role of the UN Security Council, there . . . [were]
plenty of hands raised. Many students in the Northeast sat at
their television sets and watched the antics of Russia's Yakov

Malik as President of the Council, and are eager to talk about what they saw. Television's day-by-day coverage of the Council's proceedings was one of its many services.

Now let's take a look at some pupils who are too young to know about the Security Council. A kindergarten teacher recently began to tell her five-old-olds about the pledge to the flag. To her amazement she found that the tots already knew the pledge. They had learned it while watching television!

TV at home can be an education in itself. News events spring to life as you watch things actually happening. (If you saw . . . [the recent presidential] inauguration via TV . . . do you think you will ever forget it?) Here's what one of television's supporters (Leon Levine, CBS Discussion Director) has to say:

"It will make our youngsters happier, better informed, better educated, more understanding of what the world we live in is like. It will acquaint them with the kind of people who govern us; with the plays and literature which have formed our literary heritage; with the music and dance and opera which are our culture, and with the manners and habits and speech of our people.

"Television will extend the classroom to the outside world, to the arena of the political debate, to the achievements of science, to the arena of international relations and people. Television, still in its infancy, is already doing this now and will do more."

Yes, television is moving right into the classroom, or at least into the school auditorium. [In 1950] . . . twenty-one school systems were already putting TV to work. . . . School television can operate in three ways:

First, teachers can make use of class or study hall time for viewing of regular television broadcasts. (UN programs or the opening of Congress are examples.) Second, schools and TV stations can cooperate to broadcast special programs for schools. Philadelphia, Minneapolis, Baltimore, Chicago, are among cities into the school auditorium. . . . [In 1950] twenty-one school

And third, local school systems may eventually have their own television stations—to produce their own programs and to relay other TV broadcasts into the schools.

All these offer possibilities for enriching our educational programs. Scientific demonstrations, by experts from a superbly equipped laboratory, can bring chemistry and physics to life far easier than simpler classroom experiments. History will leap from the pages of textbooks through the dramatization of past events and through the direct viewing of current events as they take place.

But what about the homework problem? How do we keep television from interfering with evening assignments?

The answer is fairly simple. At home, first things must come first. Parents and children must join together to exercise a little discipline on themselves. Of course, you don't want to miss your favorite TV variety show, or the TV film revival of *Pygmalion* or *Stagecoach* or even the crucial night baseball game. But you can arrange to get your homework done *first*. Or if there's an important math exam coming up tomorrow, TV can be skipped for one evening. We certainly shouldn't just throw up our hands helplessly before the onrush of television.

Moderation in the use of TV may be difficult for families who have just rearranged the living room furniture to make room for the shiny new TV set. Television, like many other new wonders, goes through a "fad" stage. (Radio was the same way in the 1920's. Ask your folks how many hours they spent on the crystal set trying to "get" Pittsburgh.) After television is a permanent resident in your home, you become more selective. You pay attention only to the programs that specially interest you.

The people who raise the cry of doom over television's effect on education are shortsighted. They don't recognize a many-edged educational "tool" when it is literally staring them in the face.

RADIO'S PART IN ADULT EDUCATION [9]

James A. Garfield, President of the United States in 1881, once remarked that "Next in importance to freedom and justice is popular education, without which neither justice nor freedom

[9] From "Education for Adults on the U. S. Air Waves," by Dorothy F. Greenwood, Director of Adult Programs, Radio Station KUOM, University of Minnesota. *Food for Thought.* 12:9-15. May 1952. Reprinted by permission.

can be permanently maintained." It was in making education not only common to all, but in a sense compulsory to all, that the destiny of the United States was guaranteed.

In theory, at least, the average American citizen supports the democratic concept of schoolroom education. He fails, however, to recognize that education must be dynamic and must utilize new ideas, methods, and techniques in order to achieve its ultimate goal—a well-informed, and free-thinking citizenry.

Perhaps the most flagrant example existing today is the almost universal disregard for the vast educational potentialities of the communications media which have emerged in the past half century. It is almost inconceivable that in a nation where radio, film and television have been developed to a high degree of technical proficiency, these media have not yet been creatively adapted to present-day educational needs.

The depressing history of educational radio in the United States cannot be laid at the feet of the radio industry entirely. The educational institutions, adult education agencies and the general public must share in any blame which can be attached. . . .

Educational radio for adults is an extremely flexible type of programming and can be made to include almost any field of interest. This is not a facetious statement, because educators have never committed themselves to definitions or clear descriptions of what constitutes an educational program. The general public frequently points to the discussions heard on commercial networks as "educational" broadcasting. However, these discussions usually emphasize extreme differences of opinion, do not concentrate on the identification of the problem, seldom make any analysis of why the problem exists, and rarely undertake to secure cooperative action in facing the problem. Although these programs provide some information, the main emphasis is usually on the entertainment involved when the participants try to outwit one another.

Strictly speaking, one cannot classify a discussion as an "educational" program. However, the aim frequently is to help inform the public. If there is a dearth of rational and interesting speakers who have knowledge of constructive debating techniques the radio stations can hardly be blamed for the conse-

quences. There is a great deal to be done before the adult educators and the radio stations really come to conclusions about the
place of informal education on the air-waves, and the best methods to use in order to assure some real value to listeners.

The main popular movement which has attempted to unite
adult education and radio has been the so-called radio council.
Radio councils are voluntary groups of citizens working cooperatively in the interests of all social groups in the community and
independent of influence by radio stations. Although a few
radio councils have been successful, by and large they are special
groups trying to "improve" radio, with the help of experienced
radio personnel. . . . This potentially excellent idea has been
well-nigh strangled by well intentioned do-gooders who antagonize the very people who could make the cooperative venture
valuable. A truly effective radio council would safeguard against
exploitation of their air-waves, actively help radio stations in
presenting material of value to the community, and assist the
FCC in determining the value of stations to the community.

In March 1946, the Federal Communications Commission issued a report entitled *Public Service Responsibility* of *the Broadcast Licensees*—better known as the "Blue Book". . . .

One of the main contentions of the FCC was that both the
networks and local stations were not providing adequate time for
the discussion of the significant events which shape the lives of
listeners, not to mention the peoples of the world. In the eyes of
the FCC, radio stations are held responsible for helping to build
an intelligent and informed public through programs broadcast
at good listening hours.

In spite of the fact that the FCC maintained that radio stations were not fulfilling this responsibility, the "Blue Book" regulations were not enforced. Since the great upsurge of television
in the past few years, it is probably safe to say that the radio
stations generally are doing an even poorer job in public service
than they were in 1946. Although television might be accused
of having a detrimental effect on public service radio, the fact
remains that the problem existed long before television lifted its
hungry head.

Commercial stations do not exert themselves to provide adequate broadcasting of educational material because the programs do not attract big audiences. Big audiences are required to "sell" commercial products and very few stations wish to jeopardize their income by catering to the minority of listeners who want educational programs.

Educational programs may not attract big audiences but there is no reason why they could not attract larger audiences than they do. Generally speaking the stations put little time and money into these programs, with the result that a listener has to be greatly concerned over the issue at stake in order to suffer through what is often a boring and perfunctory presentation. This is where cooperation is sorely needed. The agencies for adult education have the material but the presentation experts on the stations must have the incentive to work that material into interesting and listenable programs. . . .

[Although there] are examples of . . . important contributions made to education by commercial stations during the past few years, . . . the commercial stations are broadcasting primarily for financial gain [and] one cannot look to them for great devotion to education. But what of the educational stations? Programming policies and broadcasting facilities vary tremendously among the hundred-odd noncommercial stations in the United States. In general the education station does not buy talent; rather it makes use of the university faculty as both advisers and air talent, along with available local, national and international figures who can contribute to good programming for the com-rather it makes use of the university faculty as both advisers and usually with such low power that it reaches only a small service area. In at least one instance (Iowa State College), an educational television station is in operation, although an increasing number of educational stations have been producing programs on commercial network affiliates.

Program material and quality is especially varied in the educational field. Some stations are staffed by professional radio personnel of the highest caliber; others are almost entirely staffed by students. Some specialize in religious programs, or music, or in-school listening material. In spite of these wide variations educational stations have two things in common: a dedication to serve the public in the best way possible, and a small budget on which to operate.

Until recently most of them worked independently, each doing its best to give the community the types of programs most lacking on the commercial stations. In many cases they were originating more live broadcasts from their own studios than were the commercial stations in the area. Quite often the educational stations had the only dramatic talent available in the area and were the only stations making any effort to develop local talent. One proof that the programs were and are acceptable to the radio industry as well as the listeners is the fact that the University of Minnesota radio station KUOM has received thirty-five awards since 1940 from the Ohio Institute for Education by Radio and Television, *Variety* and *Billboard* magazines and others. The shortcomings of the educational stations were and are many, but the sincerity of purpose and the resultant programming are nothing short of phenomenal.

The isolated situation of most of these stations led a great many of the educational broadcasters to feel that they were working in a remote outpost. During the past . . . [few] years, this situation has been greatly improved through the work of the National Association of Educational Broadcasters, an organization whose membership now includes most of the country's educational stations. Formerly hampered by lack of funds, the Association recently received a grant from the Kellogg Foundation to establish a tape network.[10] Tape recordings of outstanding programs from the CBC, BBC, and member NAEB stations along with special productions, are duplicated by the headquarters of the Association at the University of Illinois. Packages of programs are then sent for distribution among a group of stations in a particular area. . . .

Thanks to the NAEB Tape Network, an educational station can now broadcast approximately eight or ten top-caliber programs each week, leaving the local staff free to concentrate more

[10] NAEB has also received substantial assistance and encouragement from the Ford Foundation.—Ed.

fully on special projects—projects which may later appear on
the network. The network not only affords relief to local stations
but also gives the opportunity for the community and the staff
to study the radio work of other stations and countries.

GOALS FOR AMERICAN BROADCASTING

EDITOR'S INTRODUCTION

What are the aims and ideals of broadcasting in the United States? Some indication is given in the first two articles in this section—one prepared by the broadcasters themselves and the other by the Federal Government agency directly concerned with broadcasting.

The remainder of this section is devoted to the views of five individuals each particularly equipped to deal with the subject. Charles Siepmann is an educator who has devoted many years to study and comment on broadcasting here and in Britain. Lyman Bryson, also an educator, has long been one of the most forward-looking men within the broadcasting industry itself. William Benton and Maurice B. Mitchell have had first-hand experience with the business end of broadcasting, and Sir William Haley, taking an over-all point of view in this article, is in the most important position of Britain's broadcasting system.

The goals set by the industry itself, by the Federal Communications Commission, and by individual observers are all commendable. How near they are to achievement must be decided, and to a large degree determined, by the reader of this volume and by the 150 million other Americans privileged to enjoy the widest variety of radio and television broadcasting available anywhere in the world.

THE BROADCASTERS' OWN STANDARDS [1]

We Believe: That American broadcasting is a living symbol of democracy; a significant and necessary instrument for main-

[1] From *Standards of Practice*, by the National Association of Radio and Television Broadcasters. The Association. Washington, D.C. 1948. p 1-8. On March 1, 1952, the Association made effective a similar but more extensive code for television broadcasters. Included was the creation of a Television Code Review Board to "review . . . all television programming, especially that of subscribers to the Television Code of NARTB; . . . and to make recommendations or prefer charges to the Television Board of Directors concerning violations and breaches of the Television Code by a subscriber."—Ed.

taining freedom of expression, as established by the First Amendment to the Constitution of the United States;

That its influence in the arts, in science, in education, in commerce and upon the public welfare, generally, is of such magnitude that the only proper measure of its responsibility is the common good of the whole people;

That it is our [i.e., the broadcasters'] obligation to serve the people in such manner as to reflect credit upon our profession and to encourage aspiration toward a better estate for all mankind; by making available to every person in America, such programs as will perpetuate the traditional leadership of the United States in all phases of the broadcasting art;

That we should make full and ingenious use of man's store of knowledge, his talents and his skills and exercise critical and discerning judgment concerning all broadcasting operations to the end that we may, intelligently and sympathetically:

Observe the properties and customs of civilized society;

Respect the rights and sensitivities of all people;

Honor the sanctity of marriage and the home;

Protect and uphold the dignity and brotherhood of all mankind;

Enrich the daily life of the people through the factual reporting and analysis of the news, and through programs of education, entertainment and information;

Provide for the fair discussion of matters of general public concern; engage in works directed toward the common good; and volunteer our aid and comfort in times of stress and emergency;

Contribute to the economic welfare of all, by expanding the channels of trade; by encouraging the development and conservation of natural resources; and by bringing together the buyer and seller through the broadcasting of information pertaining to goods and services.

Therefore, as a guide for the achievement of our purposes, we subscribe to the following standards of practice:

PROGRAM STANDARDS

News: News reporting should be factual, fair and without bias. Commentary and analyses should be clearly identified as such.

Good taste should prevail in the selection and handling of news. Morbid, sensational or alarming details not essential to the factual report, especially in connection with stories of crime or sex, should be avoided. News should be broadcast in such a manner as to avoid panic and unnecessary alarm.

Broadcasters should exercise due care in their supervision of content, format, and presentation of news broadcasts originated by them; and in their selection of newscasters, commentators and analysts.

Broadcasters should exercise particular discrimination in the acceptance and placement of advertising in news programs. Such advertising should be appropriate to the program, both as to content and presentation, and should be distinctly set apart from the news content. . . .

Political Broadcasts: Political broadcasts, or the dramatization of political issues designed to influence an election, should, if accepted, be properly identified as such.

Public Affairs and Issues: A broadcaster, in allotting time for the presentation of public questions, including those of a controversial nature, should use his best efforts to insure fair presentation. Such time should be allotted with due regard to all other elements of balanced program schedules, and to the degree of interest on the part of the public in the questions to be presented.

Discussion of controversial public issues should be presented on programs specifically intended for that purpose, and they should be clearly identified as such.

The presentation of controversial public issues should be made by properly identified persons or groups.

Freedom of expression of opinion in broadcasts of controversial issues should be carefully maintained, but the right should be reserved to refuse them for noncompliance with laws such as those prohibiting defamation and sedition.

Religious Programs: Broadcasting, which reaches men of all creeds simultaneously, should avoid attacks upon religion.

Religious programs should be presented respectfully and accurately, and without prejudice or ridicule.

Religious programs should be presented by responsible individuals, groups and organizations.

Religious programs should place emphasis on broad religious truths, excluding the presentation of controversial or partisan views not directly or necessarily related to religion or morality.

Children's Programs: Children's programs should be based upon sound social concepts and should reflect respect for parents, law and order, clean living, high morals, fair play and honorable behavior.

They should convey the commonly accepted moral, social and ethical ideals characteristic of American life.

They should contribute to the healthy development of personality and character.

There should be no appeals urging children to purchase the product in order to keep the program on the air, or which for any purpose encourage children to enter strange places or to converse with strangers.

Educational: Every radio program performs an educational function. Broadcasters should recognize the great responsibilities thus imposed, in planning their programs, to insure the most beneficial service to all listeners.

Broadcasters should cooperate with educators and with educational groups in developing improved techniques of broadcasting, as well as those processes of education best calculated to produce expert and skillful personnel.

Crime and Mystery Programs: In determining the acceptability of any program containing any element of crime, horror or mystery, due consideration should be given to the possible effect on all members of the family.

If the techniques and methods of crime are presented it should be done in such a way as not to encourage imitation; criminals should be punished, specifically or by implication; and programs which tend to make the commission of crime attractive should not be permitted.

Such programs should avoid the following subject matter:

Detailed presentation of brutal killings, torture or physical agony, horror, the use of supernatural or climactic incidents likely to terrify or excite unduly.

Episodes involving the kidnaping of children.

Sound effects calculated to mislead, shock or unduly alarm the listener.

Disrespectful portrayal of law enforcement; and characterization of officers of the law as stupid or ridiculous.

Suicide as a satisfactory solution to any problem.

General: Sound effects and expressions characteristically associated with news broadcasts (such as "bulletin," "flash," etc.) should be reserved for announcement of news, and the use of any deceptive techniques in connection with fictional events and non-news programs should be unacceptable.

When plot development requires the use of material which depends upon physical or mental handicaps it should be used in such a way as to spare the sensibilities of sufferers from similar defects.

The regular and recurrent broadcasting, in advance of sports events, of information relating to prevailing odds, the effect of which could be expected to encourage gambling should not be permitted.

Simulation of court atmosphere or use of the term "Court" in a program title should be done only in such a manner as to eliminate the possibility of creating the false impression that the proceedings broadcast are vested with judicial or official authority.

In cases of programs broadcast over multiple station facilities, the originating station should assume responsibility for conforming such programs to these Standards of Practice.

ADVERTISING STANDARDS

Advertising is the life blood of the free, competitive American system of broadcasting. It makes possible the presentation, to all the American people, of the finest programs of entertainment, information and culture.

Diligence should be exercised to the end that advertising copy accepted for broadcasting complies with pertinent Federal, state and local laws. Acceptance of advertising should be predicated upon such considerations as the integrity of the advertiser, the quality of the product, the value of service, and the validity of claims made.

In accepting advertising the broadcaster should exercise great care that he is not conveying to his audience information which is misleading, dangerous to health or character, distasteful or contrary to the proprieties and customs characteristic of his audience or in violation of business and professional ethics.

Advertising copy should contain no claims intended to disparage competitors, competing products, or other industries, professions or institutions.

Advertising copy should contain no claims that a product will effect a cure.

Good taste should always govern the content, placement or presentation of announcements. Disturbing or annoying sound effects and devices, blatant announcing and over-repetition should be avoided. . . .

Contests: Any broadcasting designed to "buy" the radio audience, by requiring it to listen in hope of reward, rather than for the quality of its entertainment should be avoided.

Contests should offer the opportunity to all contestants to win on the basis of ability and skill, rather than chance.

All contest details, including rules, eligibility requirements, opening and termination dates should be clearly and completely announced or easily accessible to the listening public; and the winners' names should be released as soon as possible after the close of the contest.

When advertising is accepted which requests contestants to submit items of product identification or other evidence of purchase of product, reasonable facsimiles thereof should be made acceptable. . . .

Premiums and Offers: Full details of proposed offers should be submitted to the broadcaster for investigation and approval before the first announcement of the offer is made to the public.

A final date for the termination of an offer should be announced as far in advance as possible.

If a consideration is required, the advertiser should agree to honor complaints indicating dissatisfaction with the premium by returning the consideration.

There should be no misleading descriptions or comparisons of any premiums or gifts which will distort or enlarge their value in the minds of the listeners.

PUBLIC SERVICE RESPONSIBILITY
OF BROADCASTERS [2]

A. ROLE OF THE PUBLIC

Primary responsibility for the American system of broadcasting rests with the licensee of broadcast stations, including the network organizations. It is to the stations and networks rather than to Federal regulation that listeners must primarily turn for improved standards of program service. The [Federal Communications] Commission, as the licensing agency established by Congress, has a responsibility to consider over-all program service in its public interest determinations, but affirmative improvement of program service must be the result primarily of other forces.

One such force is self-regulation by the industry itself, through its trade associations.

Licensees acting individually can also do much to raise program service standards, and some progress has indeed been made. Here and there across the country, some stations have evidenced an increased awareness of the importance of sustaining programs, live programs, and discussion programs. Other stations have eliminated from their own program service the middle commercial, the transcribed commercial, the piling up of commercials, etc. This trend toward self-improvement, if continued, may fur-

[2] From *Public Service Responsibility of Broadcast Licensees*, the so-called "Blue Book" issued by the Federal Communications Commission, March 7, 1946. Washington, D.C. p54-6. The portion quoted here is from the Commission's "Summary and Conclusions—Proposals for Future Commission Policy." These standards for measurement of the broadcasters' degree of "public interest" by a governmental agency continue to be a source of controversy among broadcasters. See reference to this in the article in this section by Maurice B. Mitchell, p 178-81.—Ed.

ther buttress the industry against the rising tide of informed and responsible criticism.

Forces outside the broadcasting industry similarly have a role to play in improved program service. There is need, for example, for professional radio critics, who will play in this field the role which literary and dramatic critics have long assumed in the older forms of artistic expression. It is, indeed, a curious instance of the time lag in our adjustment to changed circumstances that while plays and concerts performed to comparatively small audiences in the "legitimate" theatre or concert hall are regularly reviewed in the press, radio's best productions performed before an audience of millions receive only occasional and limited critical consideration. Publicity for radio programs is useful, but limited in the function it performs. Responsible criticism can do much more than mere promotion; it can raise the standards of public appreciation and stimulate the free and unfettered development of radio as a new medium of artistic expression. The independent radio critic, assuming the same role long occupied by the dramatic critic and the literary critic, can bring to bear an objective judgment on questions of good taste and of artistic merit which lie outside the purview of this Commission. The reviews and critiques published weekly in *Variety* afford an illustration of the role that independent criticism can play; newspapers and periodicals might well consider the institution of similar independent critiques for the general public.

Radio listener councils can also do much to improve the quality of program service. Such councils, notably in Cleveland, Ohio, and Madison, Wisconsin, have already shown the possibilities of independent listener organization. First, they can provide a much needed channel through which listeners can convey to broadcasters the wishes of the vast but not generally articulate radio audience. Second, listener councils can engage in much needed research concerning public tastes and attitudes. Third, listener councils can check on the failure of network affiliates to carry outstanding network sustaining programs, and on the local programs substituted for outstanding network sustaining programs. Fourth, they can serve to publicize and to promote outstanding programs—especially sustaining programs which at present suffer a serious handicap for lack of the vast promotional enterprise which goes to publicize many commercial programs. Other useful functions would also no doubt result from an increase in the number and an extension of the range of activities of listener councils, cooperating with the broadcasting industry but speaking solely for the interest of listeners themselves.

Colleges and universities, some of them already active in the field, have a like distinctive role to play. Together with the public schools, they have it in their power to raise a new generation of listeners with higher standards and expectations of what radio can offer.

In radio workshops, knowledge may be acquired of the techniques of radio production. There are already many examples of students graduating from such work who have found their way into the industry, carrying with them standards and conceptions of radio's role, as well as talents, by which radio service cannot fail to be enriched.

Even more important, however, is the role of colleges and universities in the field of radio research. There is room for a vast expansion of studies of the commercial, artistic and social aspects of radio. The cultural aspects of radio's influence provide in themselves a vast and fascinating field of research. . . .

B.   ROLE OF THE COMMISSION

While much of the responsibility for improved program service lies with the broadcasting industry and with the public, the Commission has a statutory responsibility for the public interest, of which it cannot divest itself. . . .

In issuing and in renewing the licenses of broadcast stations the Commission proposes to give particular consideration to four program service factors relevant to the public interest. These are: (1) the carrying of sustaining programs, including network sustaining programs, with particular reference to the retention by licensees of a proper discretion and responsibility for maintaining a well-balanced program structure; (2) the carrying of local live programs; (3) the carrying of programs devoted to the discussion of public issues, and (4) the elimination of advertising excesses.

(1) *Sustaining programs.* The carrying of sustaining programs has always been deemed one aspect of broadcast operation in the public interest. Sustaining programs . . . perform a fivefold function in (a) maintaining an over-all program balance, (b) providing time for programs inappropriate for sponsorship, (c) providing time for programs serving particular minority tastes and interests, (d) providing time for nonprofit organizations—religious, civic, agricultural, labor, educational, etc., and (e) providing time for experiment and for unfettered artistic self-expression.

Accordingly, the Commission concludes that one standard of operation in the public interest is a reasonable proportion of time devoted to sustaining programs.

Moreover, if sustaining programs are to perform their traditional functions in the American system of broadcasting, they must be broadcast at hours when the public is awake and listening. The time devoted to sustaining programs, accordingly, should be reasonably distributed among the various segments of the broadcast day. . . .

(2) *Local live programs.* The Commission has always placed a marked emphasis, and in some cases perhaps an undue emphasis, on the carrying of local live programs as a standard of public interest. The development of network, transcription, and wire news services is such that no sound public interest appears to be served by continuing to stress local live programs exclusively at the expense of these other categories. Nevertheless, reasonable provision for local self-expression still remains an essential function of a station's operation . . . and will continue to be so regarded by the Commission. In particular, public interest requires that such programs should not be crowded out of the best listening hours.

(3) *Programs devoted to the discussion of public issues.* The crucial need for discussion programs, at the local, national, and international levels alike is universally realized. . . Accordingly, the carrying of such programs in reasonable sufficiency, and dur-

ing good listening hours, is a factor to be considered in any finding of public interest.

(4) *Advertising excesses.* . . . Some stations during some or many portions of the broadcast day have engaged in advertising excesses which are incompatible with their public responsibilities, and which threaten the good name of broadcasting itself.

As the broadcasting industry itself has insisted, the public interest clearly requires that the amount of time devoted to advertising matter shall bear a reasonable relationship to the amount of time devoted to programs. . . .

In carrying out the above objectives, the Commission proposes to continue substantially unchanged its present basic licensing procedures—namely, the requiring of written application setting forth the proposed program service of the station, the consideration of that application on its merits, and subsequently the comparison of promise and performance when an application is received for a renewal of the station license.

A "BILL OF RIGHTS" FOR LISTENERS [3]

To anyone still possessed of a sense of wonder, this is an age of miracles. And of all the miracles that science has offered us, radio, "spiriting the dumb inane," is surely one of the greatest. No one, however, is likely to concede that it has yet realized the peculiar power of miracles, as Bernard Shaw defined it, namely the power "to create faith." That it can do so, and how it can do it, are now plain. Radio can reveal to us the full stature of man and his immense potentialities. It can let us see ourselves, as we are and as we may become. The hope and faith are in the latter.

Perhaps the essence of its power is that it can persuade us that we are not alone, and thus exorcise that fear which haunts us all, warps our integrity and gnaws at our resolution. Loneliness is the consequence and price of nonparticipation. Radio can

[3] From *The Radio Listener's Bill of Rights*, by Charles A. Siepmann, writer on radio and television broadcasting. Anti-Defamation League of B'nai B'rith. New York. 1948. p45-52. Reprinted by permission.

demonstrate for us the train of social consequences and the awful price we pay collectively for noncooperation. "Every man's death diminishes me, because I am involved in mankind." Radio can prove it, in programs local, national and international in scope. Such programs need not crowd out entertainment. A modest few will do. But they must be at a time when most can listen, they must be regular, they must be publicized. And they must be heard. . . . They are, as yet, infrequent and heard by none too many. . . . But we have . . . to itemize our own default in the matter and the means of our making good.

Our default stems from the three I's: from ignorance, indifference, and inertia. The cure is simple. Acquire knowledge of your rights, learn to value your rights, exercise your rights—while recognizing that every right involves a duty. It all starts, though it doesn't end, with you and me. We must bestir ourselves. But, as with most human endeavor, there are limits to what we can achieve alone and we soon become involved in group effort and achievement. Let us, however, start with what you and I can do alone.

The first step is to dispose of ignorance—in yourself and, as far as you can, in others. What must you know?

The essential knowledge you must have—and spread—about radio is the fact that it is yours. The *wavelengths of the air belong to the people of America.* Beyond possession of the air waves, you have a considerable cash investment to protect. Your purchase of a receiving set involves a capital outlay far in excess of the total capital outlay of all networks and stations. In 1947, listeners had $3 billion invested in this way. Thus [as J. H. Spingarn states in *Radio Is Yours*] "radio is no gift horse, and you have every right to look into the mouth of the loudspeaker. You definitely pay for your entertainment, and radio owes good broadcast service. You should not feel like a small boy sneaking a free peek at a ball game through a hole in the fence. You should feel more like a king in a royal box, witnessing a command performance."

Remember, next, that *every radio station is morally and legally committed to render public service.* It is your business to define, in your own terms, what constitutes essential public service. Never mind, for the moment, whether you get it. First have a mind, a point of view, about it. Know what you want, and even more what you need, to be a civilized, responsible citizen of the world. . . .

Beyond knowledge is your responsibility to care and to act. This involves becoming a good listener. Watch your listening habits. . . . Much listening as now practiced is a bad habit, bad because it is passive, uncritical, vicarious experience; a waste of precious time. Some of it is worse—a wanton escape into fantasy living, the indulgence of sentimental day dreaming. Some listeners are in this sense little better than drug addicts, shutting the mind's door on reality. . . . Here are a few suggestions [on being a good listener]:

a. *Establish your own criteria of what a well-balanced program service by a station (say, over a week) consists.* Then check your local station's program schedule and see whether it meets your specification. You can't tell how good or bad radio is until you have standards of your own to judge it by. Include among your expectations adequate reflection of the life and problems of your community and, if your station is affiliated to a network, regular carriage of the network's outstanding public service programs.

b. *Listen selectively.* Make of listening a deliberate choice, as of the books you read, the friends you see. Don't write radio off on the basis of a random sample. Check what there is. Admittedly you're ill served here. In some communities the newspapers don't even carry a radio log. Most radio logs are in any case inadequate, listing program titles without description. Has it occurred to you, however, that you can do something about this—write and complain to the station and/or the newspaper.

c. *Write to your station.* As a listener you are one of radio's shareholders. Don't be a nonvoting member. Write to your station, in praise of a program, or of programming in general where you can, in blame or protest where you must. Radio men are human. They welcome praise. They are sensitive to criticism. There is no guarantee that you will be heeded. It is certain, how-

ever, that your silence deprives you of all opportunity to make
radio your own. Correspondence does get attention. In volume
it has influence. There can be no volume if every listener discounts his individual power to influence programs by deciding,
a priori, that letters have no effect.

d. *Promote listening.* Alert others to programs you know to
be worthwhile. Get others to listen with you. Discuss what you
hear with them, in your daily encounters. If you have children,
discuss radio with them. You can influence their choice by sharp-
ening their critical faculties. Raise radio to the level of worthwhile discussion by yourself discovering—as you quickly will—
the vital principles of democratic living which it illustrates (or
belies) almost from hour to hour. Honesty, fairness, good taste,
the balance of the serious and the trivial—all these are put daily
to the test in vital contexts on the air. Remember that radio is
our major leisure avocation. In a sense, as radio is, we are. The
issue is not trivial.

But there is not one of these activities and insights which
will not be both richer and more fruitful, for being canvassed
and shared with others. Your own interest in radio will be the
greater by discovering others with like interests and a like concern
for its improvement. Make it your business, therefore, to promote discussion and action in any group to which you belong.
Are you a member of a church, a trade union, a teachers' or
parents' association? All of them have a stake in and a claim
on radio. The principles, the standards, and the causes which
they advocate are daily being advanced or retarded, bespoken or
belied, by what goes out over the air.

Ours is a society in which policy is largely influenced by
opinion-molding groups. The existence of such groups is inherent in our democratic society. They represent channels of
organized opinion. In radio, group pressure remains largely one
sided. The pressure is all on the side of the industry. This must
be remedied. The means are in your hands. Within your group,
no matter what it is, exert yourself to secure that radio receives
attention.

A good example for you is the achievement of the American
Association of University Women. Among its multifarious ac-

tivities have been . . . years of hard work on this very problem of good radio. Over eighty chapters exist whose members are active listeners and critics. Research has been jointly undertaken, and made available to all the members, revealing both the good and the bad in current radio. A regular bulletin, "The Listener," keeps members abreast of such findings, provides a forum for ideas, lists current programs of outstanding interest and reviews developments in radio that are of concern to every intelligent listener. Finding themselves not alone in interest and outlook, its members have taken heart and pressed for recognition of their collective views. Principles of program planning and demands for elimination of abuses have been presented to the radio industry and received consideration. The listener has in this instance found a collective voice and is using it with effect.

But while your group has special interests which radio can meet, it shares with other groups common interests which can be the more forcefully advanced by federated action of all such groups. Immense possibilities for making radio truly a people's platform could be realized by organizing Radio Listeners' Councils. The idea back of such councils is the pooling of interest in radio of all groups in a given community. Any council which is to be truly representative of listeners' interests must be wholly dissociated from and independent (financially or otherwise) of the radio industry. This implies no hostility to radio. It is simply a sound safeguard of true independence—of outlook and of action. The functions of a council may be thus summarized:

1. To collect and publicize essential facts on the present state of broadcasting.
2. To facilitate and encourage listening to worthwhile programs.
3. To bring pressure on stations to eliminate abuses.
4. To voice the needs of the community by preparing blueprints of worthwhile programs to be executed by a station.
5. To provide listeners with opportunities to meet and to discuss their interests in radio.
6. To alert listeners to important developments in radio by means of bulletins and circulars.

7. To represent its members' views to the Federal Communications Commission, whether with reference to matters of policy raised in public hearings before the FCC, or to the renewal of a given station's license. (Where a council is dissatisfied with a station's performance, it would do well to request the FCC to conduct local hearings on license renewal. This brings radio home to the community, as hearings in remote Washington do not.)

8. To influence not only radio, but the press, by correspondence and prepared articles on radio as a social force.

Three such councils, two of long standing, offers precedents for you to emulate—the Radio Council of Greater Cleveland, the Wisconsin Association for Better Radio Listening, and the Radio Listeners of Northern California. This last, of recent origin, but already rivaling its older associates in the vigor and enthusiasm of its work, owes its origin largely to the pioneer work previously achieved by the AAUW, referred to above. All three have gone through their growing pains and have a wealth of information to offer you on the "know-how" of organization. All issue bulletins and guides to their members, steering them to programs of proven value, keeping them informed on current happenings and garnering the needs and opinions of individual members. All of them are watchdogs for the listener, ready and able to protest the abuse of air time and to promote its better use. . . .

The growth of such councils is important. It is a community's best safeguard against the exploitation of the people's wavelengths and the surest guarantee of the consideration of its needs by radio stations. It is a means, too, of your voice and mine being heard in high quarters. You and I, perhaps, cannot go to Washington for hearings or contribute to the FCC's decision on renewal of a station's license. Our council can send its representative. Nothing, perhaps, will more affect the future of broadcasting than knowledge by a station that, when its license comes up for renewal, there will be included in the docket an accurate and critical appraisal of its services compiled by the community and presented by a listeners' council in evidence before the FCC.

Such, then, is the listener's bill of rights, a bill conceived, as every bill of rights should be, largely in terms of duties. One slogan—which we might adopt as our "commercial"—reduces the whole matter to its essence and gives us the clue to the future not only of radio but of our democracy. It is Shaw's awful warning to us, nowhere more applicable than in radio: "Get what you want, or you will grow to like what you get."

BROADCASTING AND THE "CULTIVATED MINORITY" [4]

The leaders of the broadcasting industry and the members of the cultivated public of America are failing in their responsibilities toward each other. Their attitudes toward this failure, however, are quite different. The broadcasters are mostly indifferent to the cultivated public, because it is a small and irascible minority. They prefer to deal with larger groups. The members of the minority, conscious of their superior taste and high demands, have a lot of fun deriding varieties of radio fare never intended for their attention—and dismissing, with equal amounts of dudgeon and ignorance, the whole content of broadcasting in this country. . . .

Broadcasting as a whole, as an institution, bears practically the same relation to civilization that printing does. Broadcasting is wasteful, if we think of the use of the air-waves as a miraculous privilege that ought to be kept for the beautiful and the important messages among men and nations. So is print. By far the largest part of the wood pulp that we make out of destroyed forests goes to make paper that is covered with advertising and, if you add sports gossip and comics, the residual amount of paper left for serious matters is very small. The fact is that most people are more interested in advertising and sports gossip, and comics, than in serious matters. But when the critical minority we are here discussing, the ones who carry a real responsibility for the serious concerns of civilization, speak of print, they

⁴ From "Broadcasting," by Lyman Bryson, Professor of Education, Teachers College, Columbia University; counselor on public affairs, Columbia Broadcasting System. *American Scholar*. 20:221-4. Autumn 1951. Reprinted by permission.

ignore everything but the very small part of its total product that they read.

Broadcasting judged by high standards is wasteful. Printing judged by the same standards is more so. . . .

The point of this, of course, is not to defend either form of "wastefulness," but to suggest that the differences between popular taste and cultivated taste are much the same in all the arts that have been amplified by mechanical processes, and that they are shown in the same way, i.e., by the tremendous share of the mechanical resources that are successfully monopolized by popular interests.

There are several difficulties in making the truth of this point prevail. One is the inexpugnable illusion of people of developed taste that they know what the public wants. I am quite ready to admit that the commercial broadcaster also does not know what the public wants. The field is littered with costly mistakes. The point is that his mistakes do cost him money. He does his guessing with the benefit of market research, which is quantitatively indicative, and is not trusted as anything else. He works in a system of lethal competitiveness where most scholars could not breathe. He makes his guesses in the teeth of his rivals, not before a silent and subservient class or his admiring colleagues. He frequently goes wrong. But it seems a little irrational to suppose that he is always wrong on the main point, and that the intelligentsia, with not even their reputations at stake, are always right.

To be sure, his methods of judging are largely quantitative. But it is another one of the difficulties in this problem, caused by the ignorance and indifference of the cultivated minority, that the broadcaster seldom gets much support from the special audiences that he consistently tries to include among his friendly consumers. Broadcasters on the networks and in independent stations may use quantitative measures in guessing at merely commercial audiences, but they are by no means bound by these measures. They may, incorrigibly, still hope for large numbers of auditors when they put on frankly highbrow shows. When large numbers do not listen, the programs often stay on the air if they please even a small and not very responsive part of the public.

Some critics will admit at this stage in the argument that this may be so, but the good things are at inconvenient hours. And this point of inconvenience is made also by those few of the cultivated minority who do try to appreciate and criticize honestly what is on the air for their special consumption. It does not really meet this point to say what is quite true: that most of these people will gladly go to a considerable amount of trouble to get to a theatre or concert hall on time. . . .

The most popular hours are still taken up by the most popular programs. The broadcaster cannot do much about this. He has only a front page to offer at any moment and when more than 40 per cent of all the receiving sets are tuned in, at nine in the evening, he tries to capture a good share of that fabulous audience. And he has found by experience that more people will listen to the same serious program at some other times than they will in the evening hours of family listening and network entertainment.

This is all by way of explanation, or if you like, a plea in defense. It is not very important, however, to defend the broadcasters against the intellectuals. The shoe is on the other foot. When are the intellectuals going to meet the challenge of broadcasting? I do not mean only their chance to take part in serious broadcasting; in fact, most of those who are asked do take their turns at the microphone. They are seldom as skillful at informal talking as they are in other ways of expressing ideas, but they provide a good deal of what is best in serious broadcasting, sharing that burden (or privilege) with the musicians, the workers in drama, and the news men. The unmet challenge is to know something about broadcasting as a combination of new arts, to listen seriously, and to help create serious criticism.

The newspapers and some of the weeklies have radio columns made up mostly of gossip. There are a few good professional critics of broadcasting; they often retreat into satire because they know that there is practically no public that is as much interested in reading a sober and searching criticism of a broadcast of any

kind as there is for any second-rate concert or third-rate book or
fourth-rate comedy. To say that broadcasts are not worth serious
criticism is begging the question in an especially shameful way.
Who, out of the world that constantly recreates and develops the
criticism, the canons and the appreciations of the products of
print, or the stage (also a technological device) or musical instruments, has ever suggested a list of canons for any form of
broadcasting? Most of the wisdom of the world has been developed and communicated in talk, after print as well as in the ages
before. Who has ever suggested the standards of broadcast talk?
The drama of disembodied voices and music is certainly not the
same as the drama of either the flicker in two dimensions or the
stage in three. Who has told us how to begin to measure excellence in either the documentary of force or the drama of created
emotional themes? . . .

The challenge to the members of the cultivated minority that
broadcasting offers is that they shall take the trouble—some of
them at least, while the others wait—to find out what is on the
air and then to criticize it not mercifully but intelligently, and
with the slowly acquired expertness that makes criticism valuable.
Vigorous, severe and systematic criticism is needed, and the blun-
derbuss will no longer do the work. That kind of shooting is
too easy. You are bound to hit something, but it is not likely
to be the proper target. The cultivated reader of books gives his
time to those that pretend to have some meaning in his world
of ideas, and criticizes them on relevant performance. We need
critics of broadcasting, in all its diverse forms, who will choose
their targets as carefully, and use weapons of precision.

This will not change all broadcast programs, now or ever,
into what the critics want, any more than reviews and comments
on books diminish or improve most of what comes off the
presses. But it will get for those who want better things at least
as large a share of the product of broadcasting as equally fastid-
ious consumers now get from print. A little straight thinking
and informed demand might get them more. And it will sustain
and encourage the artists and producers in radio who are moved
by the same desires as move the makers of great things in print
or elsewhere. Potential great audiences and potential great art

come into reality together by interaction and by mutual stimulation in good faith.

THREE ROADS TO TV'S SALVATION [5]

I fear . . . that . . . American television is about to take the . . . road to trivialization—with our TV stations devoting their good viewing hours to vying with a few salable program stereotypes, for the same lowest-common-denominator of audience interest, all in behalf of fifteen or twenty big sponsors. That has been the road of radio, a road which, on the whole, is a dismal one, in spite of the fact that the medium has brought entertainment and escape to tens of millions of bored, lonesome, or dreary lives.

It seems to me that there are three possible developments that might, in combination, save TV from treading the same road. The first is that the commercial television networks and license-holders will learn, or can be persuaded, that it is in their own interest to devote more and better time to educational and public service programs (let us say, for example, 7 P.M. to 9 P.M. three nights a week for adult education and public service); or that stations will be required to develop standards and adhere to them, as a condition of securing or retaining their licenses.

The second hopeful development would be a new system of telecasting, competitive with the present system which is dependent wholly on advertising revenue—a new system in which the station operator would produce programs for those willing to pay a fee.

The third is the operation of TV stations by educational institutions. . . .

The experts estimate that within five years advertisers will spend at least $1 billion a year to buy TV time and program talent. I have no doubt that the network executives are busy drafting "codes" for good programming, and that they are dis-

[5] From "Television with a Conscience," by former Senator William Benton (Democrat, Connecticut); formerly Vice President of the University of Chicago and Assistant Secretary of State. *Saturday Review of Literature.* 34:7-8+. August 25, 1951. Reprinted by permission.

cussing public service programs. There are many able and remarkable men in this fast moving, competitive industry. I have
warned my friends in the industry that they face a storm of public protest if they surrender completely to triviality, and many of
them realize it.

But I am not optimistic about their efforts. I have seen codes
and good intentions before. . . .

In 1935 I sold out my interest in the advertising agency of
Benton and Bowles. We had been the biggest single customer of
NBC, and later of CBS as well. I became a part-time vice president of the University of Chicago, with the hope of developing
educational programs on the radio networks. At the time I left
the university to become Assistant Secretary of State in 1945, the
university had two such programs, "The Human Adventure," on
Mutual, and "The University of Chicago Round Table," on
NBC. But I had failed, miserably, in the goal I had set for myself—and for radio. These programs, like other so-called educational and public service programs, had been kicked around by
the networks, shifted again and again to new time periods, or
killed.

Comparing what was known about educational programming
to what was done about it, in 1940 the networks were doing a
far poorer job than in 1930; in 1950 they were doing a far
poorer job than in 1940. The commercial pressure toward trivialization in radio has proved irresistible. What is there to resist it
in TV?

Studying today's TV, the Federal Communications Commission found that in a "composite week" in 1950 only 3 per cent
of all commercial programs were of an "educational type." Another 3 per cent were discussion programs. Less than 1 per cent
were religious.

In another study Professor Dallas Smythe of the University
of Illinois and Professor Donald Horton of the University of
Chicago monitored all programs on the seven TV stations in
metropolitan New York for one week in January. . . . [1951]
They found that, exclusive of news and homemaking programs,
only 3 per cent of all TV time could be classified as "informational," 2 per cent of TV's time went to discussion of public

issues and 1 per cent to religion. "A clear majority of the time," they reported, "was devoted to entertainment programs with relatively low or perhaps negative survival value for the individual viewer or for society." New York is the area which has had the most experience in programming and which now points the way for the rest of the country. Its pattern is disturbingly similar to radio's. It is not a happy prospect for TV throughout America. Yet Professor Charles Siepmann of New York University fears that "we may now be witnessing a peak in television's service to a variety of tastes," since the program producers have not yet settled on a handful of formulas, as radio has.

The magazine *TV* monitored all "crime shows" on the seven television stations in the Los Angeles area for the first week of May . . . [1951]. They found that close to a thousand crimes took place on the TV screens, the great majority of them on children's programs. "Seventy per cent of all programming televised specifically for children was based on crime," says the magazine. Many of these programs were reruns of movie "westerns." There may be argument as to just how deleterious these programs are, but no one can argue that television is living up to its educational potential on any such formula—especially when we remember that children are now spending more time watching television than they spend in school.

These programming studies . . . give substance to my contention that commercial television, if it is allowed to mushroom along the lines of commercial radio, without guidance from Congress or from organized public opinion, will never remotely do the great and urgent educational and public service job required by the times.

My second possibility is much more exciting and promising. It does not put its faith in begging an hour or two a day from commercial TV—a crumbs-off-the-table approach. It calls for subscription television—putting a "box office" or a "tuition fee" at the receiving end of television. And why not a system in which the viewer orders and pays for what he gets—without any advertising whatsoever? Such a system could and should be developed wholly within the American theory of private competitive broadcasting, just as the *Reader's Digest*, which carries no advertising, is completely consistent with the theory of American magazine publishing.[6] . . .

The third possibility for realizing the educational and public service potential of television lies in the development of stations operated by educational institutions. The FCC has made provision for these. . . .

I wonder how many citizens of the United States—including all who pride themselves on their interest in the educational system and all the parents who worry about what television is doing to their children—know whether a channel for education has been reserved by the FCC in their own areas. . . .

If your community has been awarded a channel by the FCC, what steps are being taken to claim it? How many months—or years—will your community need to reach a decision and arrange the financing, through the school board, the state legislature, the local college, or otherwise? The FCC suggests it will hold these educational reservations open for a reasonable period. But remember that the FCC is likely to be under constant pressure from importunate commercial applicants.

Or perhaps your school system, or a consortium of civic groups, would do better to apply for a commercial license, on a not-for-profit basis, in the expectation of carrying sponsored entertainment programs part of the day in order to finance educational programs the rest of the day. If so, that calls for an immediate decision, and a prompt presentation to the FCC. Indeed, it may already be too late. . . .

Two taunts have been hurled at the hopeful television educators. One is, "Look what happened in radio." It's true that in the 1920's well over a hundred educational institutions or boards were awarded choice radio channels. Most of these were finally relinquished to commercial operators when the educators wouldn't or couldn't use them. Educators learn slowly.

However, I cannot accept the analogy between radio and TV. Educators learn very slowly, but they do learn. Television . . . is uniquely adapted to education. As John Crosby, the New York *Herald Tribune's* radio and television critic, points out,

---

[6] See selection on subscription television, "Pay as You Look," p25-30.—Ed.

television has five times the "wallop" of radio, and it requires, and gets, five times the attention. Attention is the indispensable element in education.

The second taunt is, "Where is the money coming from?" That is the same kind of taunt which was hurled a hundred years ago against the dream of free public education for all children.

If the promise is as great as I think it is, the money will be found. The American people believe in education. They spend perhaps $5 billion a year for it today. Once they have been shown the power of television in education, I cannot believe they will deny it to themselves or to their children.

[In early 1951] . . . three foundations, the Ford, Kellogg, and Sloan Foundations . . . appropriated a total of over $2 million for the development of educational radio and TV. This is just "seed-money."

A main source of money may be appropriations by state and local governments. . . .

Another method for financing educational stations could develop if the FCC would change its formula on "noncommercial educational stations." The formula should permit "noncommercial stations" to earn a profit—for philanthropic ends. So-called educational stations should be permitted to carry entertainment programs sponsored by advertisers part of the day to earn profits to finance educational programs the rest of the day. This is the plan used by the only educational TV station now on the air, at Iowa State University, which holds a commercial license.

The third method is the "subscription" method I have already mentioned. One of my former associates at the University of Chicago has calculated that some universities could finance their year-round TV programming and even offer it free simply by withholding exclusive rights to telecasts of football games and applying the subscription technique.

What are the chances for any of my three possibilities—the full blown creation of educational stations, the development of subscription television, and the hoped for flowering of the commercial conscience—to save TV from the road to trivialization? Students of the question assure me that the answer lies less in new Federal legislation than in "the dynamics of our society." This means that the reforms can't happen unless the public makes them happen, and keeps making them happen.

PROVIDING WHAT THE PUBLIC WANTS [7]

Consider the problem of the broadcast and TV station operator. He has a bear by the tail. He operates the most potent communications force that civilization has ever known. Under our system of business life, he has to operate this force as a solvent business. No profit—no radio, no TV. And it often seems to him that every obstacle ever conceived to plague and harass a businessman is put across his path. . . .

The broadcaster has never accepted Government interference in radio in any sense except for the simple separation of stations in the spectrum. He goes along with that, and that's all. The complexities of applying for the use of one of the radio frequencies, the terrible expense, the intimate inspection of his means and his past habits and connections, have always infuriated and embarrassed him. He sees the newspaperman, the book and the magazine publisher, even the irresponsible pulp publisher or pamphleteer, set up in business beside him in all freedom while he undergoes what seems to him a contemptuous public inspection conducted by a Government agency.

The broadcaster generally believes that once the FCC has exercised its traffic function, only the opinion of the public should further guide him in the operation of his station. He points to the knob on every radio set which permits listeners to "stop the music" at will. He feels that this is censorship in its truest sense—individual selection or rejection on the basis of interest and suitability.

He has watched with increasing horror as the FCC steadily and persistently assumed—so it seems to him—that its licensing powers could only be diligently and properly discharged if it also sought to control the content of the station program schedule. Every broadcaster — indeed, every sensible person — knows that

[7] From "It's Still a Business," by Maurice B. Mitchell, General Manager, Associated Program Service, division of the Muzak Corporation. *Saturday Review of Literature,* 34:25+, November 3, 1951. Reprinted by permission.

when this happens we will have ceased to have effective private enterprise in the field of radio and TV.

The industry cites the attempt to take control of radio away from the broadcasters when in 1946 the FCC published the famous Blue Book, which simply took the position that a station which, in the opinion of the Commission, was "too commercial" might well have its license revoked. But who was to decide which stations were "too commercial"? The FCC. And was a cultural program, a symphony concert a public service? Not if it was sponsored, the Commission would readily contend.

The Blue Book is history. Its threat was smashed by aroused broadcasters. Yet it will never be forgotten, because the broadcaster eternally senses the desire on the part of government, of ill-advised "do-gooders," to sneak over a knockout punch. . . .

Year after year . . . the public does not look to radio for more of the kinds of programs its critics say it should feature. The facts show that people don't want them. They won't listen to them. They won't watch them.

And the broadcaster knows that if he tries to force his audience to listen to programs they don't want, there will soon be no audience, and maybe no radio.

Sometimes he wonders whether there shouldn't be another "freedom" added to the list of new ones we've discovered lately: freedom from culture. He thinks that many of his listeners would welcome it.

Radio may not be all we want it to be—what is, anyhow?— but in its present state it is a communications force so vital to the nation that anything that would tend to weaken it seems to the radio industry only to be classed as sabotage. I have often heard radio men remark that our enemies can do no more effective piece of damage to this nation's readiness and vitality than to jam our radio stations—not electronically from outside as they do with the Voice of America—but culturally, from within, by simply loading its program schedules with "helpful educational talks and discussions," material that they are persuaded would surely reduce its effectivenesss in quickly reaching masses of the people.

Broadcasters—and the public—are getting pretty tired of all this fuss over something that is liked and used. Listen to this composite broadcaster:

"I've been through this for years. It's always the same. Somebody decides that people aren't getting enough culture. It's easier to get at me than at the newspaper or the book or magazine publishers because I've got that FCC license renewal hanging over my head, so they pin the job on me. Sure, I'm afraid I'll lose my license, my business and my investment with it—what good is a radio transmitter without a license?—so I start loading up with all this cultural stuff. Trouble is, the only people who want it are the crackpots who threatened me—and even they don't listen to it. They're too busy trying to uplift everybody else. So I lose a lot of my listeners and my advertisers get sore and switch back to the newspapers, where they just give people what they want to read. What does this accomplish, anyhow?"

Here's another:

"I've tried. I built a radio station in this city because I felt that the stations already here weren't catering to the tastes of a segment of the audience—the cultural people, the educated ones, the opinion-forming group. I figured I could supply their needs and even raise the cultural level of some of the others who might occasionally listen to my station. I worked with the universities, the little theatre groups, the local musical clubs, with other cultural groups. I programmed discussions and talks and lectures. I almost lost my shirt. I'm all through investing in culture that nobody wants. Now I program music — good and bad — and news, and if I'm lucky eventually I'll get my losses back. . . ."

In the short three decades of commercial radio, station operators have seen a tremendous growth in the national literacy rate, a steadily increasing curve of interest in music, the theatre, the other arts—in all those things labeled "cultural." They believe that, without receiving much credit for the job and indeed without having consciously tried to achieve the effect, radio has been primarily responsible for this acceleration in public awareness. They have a feeling that further development along these lines will occur, as it has in the past, through sheer force of public interest and preference. They do not believe that you can capture men's minds, or uplift them for that matter, through legislation. They have faith in the people, and the people have faith in radio.

FREEDOM—BROADCASTING'S BASIC NECESSITY [8]

The fundamental problem of broadcasting within a democracy is to reconcile freedom with standards. . . .

That . . . [this problem] should be examined only in relation to broadcasting within democracies may seem an arbitrary limitation. In fact, it is not. Where broadcasting is carried on under governments other than democracies . . . [the problem does] not exist. To an absolute monarch, a dictator, an oligarchy, or a witch doctor, the microphone presents no dilemmas. At least, no ethical or moral ones. The particular responsibilities of broadcasting may be seen in this fact. It implies that the first duty of broadcasting among free peoples is itself to be free. . . .

[Yet] there is always some point at which the climate of even the most civilized opinion in each generation considers that liberty degenerates into license. Both the hope and the despair of mankind lie in the fact that it is never a fixed point. The struggle of the ages sees it pushed now forward, now back. Broadcasting in democracies, being in the last analysis publicly controlled—in the United States by the fact that the entire revenue depends upon the sponsors; in Great Britain by more complex processes— can never be far ahead of the foremost battle line. What we have to consider . . . is the nature of the forces operating against its taking its rightful place in the van.

The first force is that . . . in every age liberty is a relative thing. There is therefore the need to make a just equation between the proper climate of public opinion which keeps liberty the right side of what is considered as license and the natural reaction of the great majority of men and women that seeks to stifle the new and the, at first, uncomfortable, whether it be in politics, religion, culture, or art. This reaction can masquerade

[8] From "What Standards for Broadcasting?" by Sir William Haley, Director-General of the British Broadcasting Corporation. *Measure*. 1:209-21. Summer 1950. Reprinted by permission.

as climate of opinion, lazily refusing to examine the newcomer, and using the great power of public opinion to enforce its tenets. In such circumstances it has to be resisted.

The second force where broadcasting is concerned lies in the fact that intolerance is not the prerogative of certain governments. It can be displayed by sponsors, by mass opinion acting through other channels, by established institutions, or by powerful minorities—and from any of these sources can be made to masquerade as the public interest.

The third force is the modern complication that sincere friends of liberty are convinced she has to be protected against herself. We have to face up to the fact that there are powerful forces in the world today misusing the privileges of liberty in order to destroy her. The question must be asked, however, whether suppression of information or opinion is the true defense. . . .

No debate is ever permanently won by shutting one's ears or by even the most Draconian policy of silencing opponents. The debate must be won. And it must be won with full information. Where there are lies, they must be shown for what they are. Where there are errors, they must be refuted. It would be a major defeat if the enemies of democracy forced us to abandon our faith in the power of informed discussion and so brought us down to their own level. Mankind is so constituted, moreover, that if, where expression and discussion are concerned, the enemies of liberty are met with a denial of liberty, many men of good will will come to suspect there is something in the proscribed doctrine after all. Erroneous doctrines thrive on being expunged. They die if exposed. . . .

Freedom in broadcasting must be maintained to the uttermost limits within the climate of public opinion. Broadcasters should be vigilant and vigorous in resisting any attempts at encroachment upon that freedom from without. They must be equally vigilant and vigorous at resisting encroachments from within. . . .

The definition of standards is perhaps the most difficult of all the tasks those in charge of broadcasting can be asked to undertake. . . . Standards are of two kinds. There are first the standards to be applied in each particular department of broadcasting. To take perhaps the simplest instance: how low shall be the comedy which is allowed on the air? Or consider news bulletins: in broadcast news, a balance must be struck between what is important and generally uninteresting and what is exciting but trivial. This is a very real problem when it is realized that even a fifteen-minute bulletin has not as many words as two columns in a newspaper, and experience has shown that the average mind cannot retain information from a bulletin which lasts longer. Every new bulletin must therefore be compiled according to some scale of values. . . .

When we turn to culture, music, or esthetics, the consequences to national life and happiness may be almost equally powerful. A people not brought up to seek and to distinguish goodness, beauty, truth, will be poor indeed whatever other riches they may have. Here values are never constant. It is not only the new that has to be appraised; but the old must also be constantly reassessed. It may seem unbelievable that an age will ever come that will not listen to Beethoven. It is worth remembering that although Bach's genius was generally acknowledged in his lifetime, his work suffered an almost total eclipse from his death in 1750 until Mendelssohn revived it in 1829. The Greeks had to be rediscovered at the Renaissance. There are great movements, as apart from fashions, in esthetics. Broadcasting, while satisfying the needs of its time at any particular moment must at all times hold to the enduring values, not deserting the gold of yesterday for the chromium-plate of today; not letting the "masterpieces" oust the classics; and at the same time not falling into the opposite error of refusing a hearing to the new because it is so different from the old.

Standards in this sense, therefore, are a matter of taste and range. The range must be as wide as possible. The taste must be sure because it is based on principles and not on prejudice.

The second kind of standards are those applied to broadcasting as a whole. Assuming that the standards in all the different spheres that broadcasting can serve are right, there remains the question of the proportion to be maintained between the times allotted to all those various spheres. The narrow range of mass taste mentioned above operates against this second category of standards more powerfully than against the first. There are those, of course, who say that broadcasting need have no educational mission and no social purpose. If that is agreed, it is true the problem is reduced to a minimum, though minorities would still be entitled to their due. But looking at the world today and realizing that the one hope of mankind is that one day it shall become adult, civilized, and educated; that in fact the survival of democracy depends on this; appreciating the valuable, cumulative educational instrument broadcasting has in its power to be (even if only by being the greatest signpost to other quicker and surer means of education); can this responsibility possibly be let go by default? The duty of leadership in raising taste and inculcating a regard for values should be so apparent as to allow only one answer.

Viewed from this aspect the standards of any broadcasting system may be broadly judged by the seriousness of its output as a whole. No one would want broadcasting to be confined completely to serious programs. The wisest men are the better for relaxation or laughter. The less wise even more so. There is in any case little danger of that happening. But there is a real danger that broadcasting may end up with completely trivial programs. There are critics who hold that in some places this has already happened.

Given the diversity of broadcasting's material, remembering the need for the greatest possible freedom at the microphone, having regard to the Gresham's Law [of the bad driving out the good] that operates in culture, entertainment, and information owing to the present broad base of the social and educational pyramid in almost every modern community, how are standards nevertheless to be ensured?

There are some, of course, who say that all that is required is perfect freedom and that standards can look after themselves. The hollowness of this can be demonstrated in various ways. First, to take an extreme case, it is considered everywhere necessary to have laws to exclude blasphemy, obscenity, and so on. Secondly, the weight of public opinion does not stop the kind of newspapers that generally have the largest circulations from hav-

ing them. And when the microphone has been used to build up
a number of people into unofficial public oracles, those who have
come to the top in popularity have not always been notable for
their judgment, wisdom, or taste.

The matter is much more complex. It is the need to allow
the microphone to every proper form of expression, no matter
how outlandish, or new, or novel, or trite, or banal, or outmoded,
or silly it may appear to be, and without injuring freedom to see
that the spurious does not drive out the true, that the humbug
does not supersede the genuine, that the result of the greatest
possible free-for-all is not a still greater lowering of values.

That it can be done there is no doubt. But it will only be
done if it is a conscious process. This means that there must be
a maximum of freedom, but a conscious curbing of laissez-faire.
There must be a more explicit recognition of the true function
of broadcasting. And in the light of that recognition it must be
staffed with the kind of people who will make its service their
career and will forward its purposes. Broadcasting, despite all its
diversity, must be regarded primarily as an educational medium,
with a cumulative effect and a progressive aim. There must be
recruited to it the highest caliber of men and women in all walks
of life that can possibly be attracted. They must be kept fresh,
eager, questing, animated both by a faith in the things that matter
and a spirit of intellectual doubt that is constantly seeking to
determine what those things will prove to be. Through everything they must be prepared to hold fast to the ancient moral
values. These are well established. They derive from Greece,
Rome, and the Holy Land. They are the basis of our civilization
whether we apply them or not. Those in charge of broadcasting
must use them as reagents on everything claiming admission to
the microphone, denying to none the right to pass the test.

They must be prepared to make mistakes and to profit by
their mistakes. For much that has been said earlier about the
weakness of broadcasting is also one of its greatest assets where
experiment is concerned. If no overwhelming abiding good can
be done by a single broadcast, it is true also that the single broadcast, however bad, can do little abiding harm. As a matter of
fact, far too much fuss is made in almost every country about the

occasional bad broadcast. It is not in the individual bad broadcast that the danger to standards lies. It is in the trend of broadcasting as a whole. Any single bad broadcast should be judged mainly in the light of how it affects that trend. But it is the trend as a whole that should be ceaselessly, rigorously, unsparingly examined. . . .

Of the encroachments on broadcasting's freedom which may come from within itself, one of the most dangerous and most insidious . . . is broadcasting's increasing subservience to time. The clock has become a tyrant. Hour broadcasts have been cut to half-hours, even half-hours are sometimes outnumbered by those of fifteen minutes. The demands of the material are denied; the crudest and cruelest injury is done to works of art; trimming, expurgation, cutting, gutting go to limits that offend all sense and taste.

The overriding reason is, of course, the fear that the listener may switch off. He or she *must* be kept at the loudspeaker. Therefore, quick and constant changes are everything. All other considerations must be subordinated to the need for maintaining attention. The truth is that it is not attention that is thus maintained. It is a half-ear background listening that may pick up a sponsor's message, a comedian's jokes, or an audience's applause, but will retain little of more serious purpose. . . .

Freedom, diversity, standards, purpose, time. These may seem a strange assortment of requirements to make of broadcasting. Its needs are generally expressed in other terms. But its duty, however expressed, should come in essence to one thing. Broadcasting should play its part in bringing about the reign of truth. Truth is here used in the widest sense.

Truth may be said to be ever and never in danger. If men and women fear more for truth today than ever before, is it not because they have now come to recognize more than ever that in the sum of all its aspects it is the life force of their whole ethic and civilization? In a world beset by disintegrating forces, truth is bearing the brunt of the attack. If it fails, all the other values free men hold dear must perish.

BIBLIOGRAPHY

An asterisk (*) preceding a reference indicates that the article or a part of it has been reprinted in this book.

BIBLIOGRAPHIES

Rose, Oscar. Radio broadcasting and television. 120p. H. W. Wilson Company. New York. '47.
Broadcasting. 40:579-81. Ja. 15, '51. Radio and TV reference books and publications. Agnes Law.
English Journal. 38:295-7. My. '49. Selected bibliography on radio and television for teachers. S. G. Gilburt.
United States Office of Education Bulletin. 1948, no 17:1-33. '48. Radio and television bibliography. G. G. Broderick.

BOOKS AND PAMPHLETS

Bryson, Lyman. Time for reason about radio. 127p. George W. Stewart, Publisher, Inc. 109 E. 39th St. New York 16. '48.
Chester, Giraud, and Garrison, G. R. Radio and television: an introduction. 550p. D. Appleton-Century. New York. '50.
    Bibliography.
Columbia Broadcasting System. Close-up; a picture of the men and methods that make CBS television. CBS. New York. '49.
Craig, J. W. Television's role in distribution and defense. In Report of 22d annual Boston Conference on Distribution. p64-8. Boston Chamber of Commerce. Boston. '50.
Crosby, John. Out of the blue. 301p. Simon and Schuster. New York. '52.
*Cunningham & Walsh, Inc. Videotown-V; fifth annual census of television and its effect on family life. 28p. Cunningham and Walsh, Inc. 40 E. 34th St. New York 16. '52.
Dunlap, O. E. Dunlap's radio and television almanac. 211p. Harper and Bros. New York. '51.
Dunlap, O. E. Understanding television. 128p. Greenberg. New York. '48.
*Federal Communications Commission. Public service responsibility of broadcast licensees. 59p. Supt. of Docs. Washington 25, D.C. '46.
Fellows, H. E. Advertising stopped at 10 o'clock this morning. 11p. National Association of Radio and Television Broadcasters. 1771 N St., N.W. Washington 6, D.C. '52.

Fellows, H. E. Testimony on political broadcasting before Senate Committee on Rules and Administration, April 24, 1952. 11p. mimeo. National Association of Radio and Television Broadcasters. 1771 N St., N.W. Washington 6, D.C. '52.

Fellows, H. E. Testimony on program content before the House Interstate and Foreign Commerce Committee, June 26, 1952. 10p. mimeo. National Association of Radio and Television Broadcasters. 1771 N St. N.W. Washington 6, D.C. '52.

Halpern, N. L. Harnessing the television giant for theatre television. 15p. Theatre Owners of America, Inc. 1501 Broadway. New York 18. '50.

Halpern, N. L. What about television and the movies? 10p. Theatre Owners of America. 1501 Broadway. New York 18. '50.

Hardy, R. W. Testimony on broadcasting practices and procedures, before House Interstate and Foreign Commerce Committee, September 16, 1952. 9p. mimeo. National Association of Radio and Television Broadcasters. 1771 N St., N.W. Washington 6, D.C. '52.

Hennock, F. B. Educational television can strengthen American democracy; address delivered before National Jewish Welfare Board, Detroit, Michigan, May 2, 1952. 4p. mimeo. Federal Communications Commission. Washington 25, D.C. '52.

Hennock, F. B. Educational television nears reality in Los Angeles; address delivered before the Los Angeles Educational Television Committee, September 8, 1952. 5p. mimeo. Federal Communications Commission. Washington 25, D.C. '52.

Hennock, F. B. Educational television: new force in Houston; address delivered at University of Houston (Texas), August 30, 1952. 6p. mimeo. Federal Communications Commission. Washington 25, D.C. '52.

Joint Committee on Educational Television. Editorials on education television. 6p. mimeo. The Committee. 1785 Massachusetts Ave. N.W. Washington 6, D.C. '52.

Joint Committee on Educational Television. TV channels for education. 32p. The Committee. 1785 Massachusetts Ave., N.W. Washington 6, D.C. '52.

Lazarsfeld, P. F. and Kendall, P. L. Radio listening in America. 178p. Prentice-Hall. New York. '48.

Merton, R. K. and others. Mass persuasion. 210p. Harper and Bros. New York. '47.

Miller, Justin. Statement on "Mayflower rule" before Federal Communications Commission. 32p. National Association of Radio and Television Broadcasters. 1771 N St., N.W. Washington 6, D.C. '48.

Miller, Justin. Textbooks and TV. 32p. National Association of Radio and Television Broadcasters. 1771 N St., N.W. Washington 6, D.C. '51.

National Association of Radio and Television Broadcasters. Experts look at radio and TV. 58p. The Association. 1771 N St., N.W. Washington 6, D.C. '52.

*National Association of Radio and Television Broadcasters. Standards of practice for American broadcasters. 10p. The Association. 1771 N St., N.W. Washington 6, D.C. '48.

National Association of Radio and Television Broadcasters. Television code. 10p. The Association. 1771 N St., N.W. Washington 6, D.C. '52.

National Broadcasting Company. NBC radio and television broadcast standards. 46p. The Company. 30 Rockefeller Plaza. New York 20. '51.

National Broadcasting Company. Television today; its impact on people and products. 67p. The Company. 30 Rockefeller Plaza. New York 20. '51.

Olsen, O. J. Education on the air, 1951. 519p. Ohio State University Press. Columbus, Ohio. '52.

New edition issued annually.

Radio Corporation of America. The campaign comes to 18,000,000 whistle stops. [An advertisement published in the New York Times. p. 13. Ag. 19, '52, and elsewhere.]

Rankin, F. A. Who gets the air; U. S. broadcaster in world affairs. 64p. National Association of Radio and Television Broadcasters. 1771 N St., N.W. Washington 6, D.C. '49.

Sarnoff, David. Year-end statement. 11p. Radio Corporation of America. 30 Rockefeller Plaza. New York 20. '52.

Seldes, Gilbert. Great audience. 299p. Viking Press. New York. '50.

*Shayon, R. L. Television and our children. 94p. Longmans, Green and Co. New York. '51.

*Siepmann, C. A. Radio listeners' bills of rights: democracy, radio and you. 52p. Anti-Defamation League of B'nai Brith. 212 Fifth Ave. New York 10. '48.

Siepmann, C. A. Radio, television and society. 410p. Oxford University Press. New York. '50.

Siepmann, C. A. Radio's second chance. 282p. Little, Brown and Co. Boston. '46.

Summers, R. E. America's weapons of psychological warfare. (Reference Shelf, v23, no4) 206p. H. W. Wilson Co. New York. '51.

United States. House of Representatives. Subcommittee of the Committee on Interstate and Foreign Commerce. Final report. 14p. Supt. of Docs. Washington 25, D.C. '52.

United States. House of Representatives. Subcommittee of the Committee on Interstate and Foreign Commerce. Investigation of radio and television programs. 493p. Supt. of Docs. Washington 25, D.C. '52.

United States. Office of Education. First draft of a declaration of people's rights in radio and television. Franklin Dunham. mimeo. Federal Security Agency. Washington 25, D.C. '51.

*United States. Supreme Court. Official reports of Supreme Court, v343, U.S. no3—v344, U.S., no2 [cases adjudged in Supreme Court at October term 1951 and 1952 (opinions May 5—December 22, 1952)]. Superintendent of Documents. Washington 25, D.C. '53.

*Walker, P. A. Address delivered at the Annual Education Congress, Harrisburg, Pa., October 2, 1952. 10p. mimeo. Federal Communications Commission. Washington 25, D.C. '52.

Walker, P. A. Job ahead for educational TV. Address delivered at the WOI-TV Television Workshop, Ames, Iowa, August 18, 1952. mimeo. Federal Communications Commission. Washington 25, D.C. '52.

*White, Llewelyn. American radio. 260p. University of Chicago Press. Chicago. '47.

*Williams, A. N. Listening. 152p. University of Denver Press. Denver. '48.

Willis, E. E. Foundations in broadcasting; radio and television. 439p. Oxford University Press. New York. '51.
    Bibliography.

Wilson, L. A. and others. Television, education's greatest challenge. 20p. University of the State of New York. Albany, N.Y. '51.

PERIODICALS

Advertising Age. 22:47-8, 39-40. Jl. 23-30, '51. High school students' TV habits. B. M. Bradway.
    Condensed in Education Digest. 17:10-12. O. '51.

Advertising Agency. p52-5+. O. '50. How will television affect newspapers? R. D. Levitt.

Advertising Agency. p 16+. Ag. '51. Five reasons why radio isn't dead. C. H. Wolfe.

Advertising Agency. p74-5+. S. '52. Legal problems created by TV. J. L. Ames.

*American Bar Association Journal. 38:15-18+. Ja. '52. Justice and TV. W. T. Gossett.

*American City. 65:136-7. D. '50. WYNC. Irving Luscombe.

American City. 67:149. S. '52. San Antonio goes all out for radio and television programs.

American Federationist. p7-8. D. '50. TV for the people. George Meany.

American Magazine. 153:21+. Ap. '52. TV and the 1952 election. John Crosby.

American Mercury. 74:114-19. F. '50. Television giant in the living room. Calder Willingham.

*American Scholar. 17:221-4. Spring '48. Broadcasting. Lyman Bryson.

American Scholar. 17:224-7. Spring '48. American radio; what is wrong with it. M. S. Young.

American Scholar. 20:447-54. Autumn '51. Television; how bad can it be? M. S. Young.
    Reply. 21:227+. Spring '52. H. F. Reeves.
American School Board Journal. 123:21-2. D. '51. Television in high schools. R. E. Helmick.
American School Board Journal. 123:23. D. '51. Dangers of education by television. C. J. Dintelman.
American School Board Journal. 125:29-32+. O. '52. Television and the schools. Ralph Steetle and Elaine Exton.
*Annals of the American Academy of Political and Social Science. 280: 116-24. Mr. '52. Radio and television and ethical standards. F. C. Gruber.
Atlantic Monthly. 189:44-7. My. '52. TV gold rush. Trudie Osborne.
Broadcasting. 39:61-168. O. 16, '50. Two exciting decades of radio.
Bus Transportation. p66-7. N. '50. They shall have music. Frank Otwell.
Business Week. p 120-2. N. 10, '51. Magazines: is TV a threat?
Business Week. p 182+. My. 17, '52. Educational TV is coming.
Business Week. p31. My. 31, '52. He who rides must listen.
Business Week. p58. Je. 21, '52. Pay-as-you-go TV.
Business Week. p38+. Jl. 19, '52. New study on "Videotown."
Business Week. p46-8. Ag. 9, '52. Hollywood learns how to live with TV.
Business Week. p 172. S. 20, '52. Wisconsin runs a radio network
*Business Week. p38+. S. 27, '52. Does television really spoil the gate?
*Changing Times. p32-3. N. '50. Radio station that dares to be different.
Christian Century. 68:584-5. My. 9, '51. Back of the Kefauver TV show. A. M. Motter.
Collier's. 128:18-19+. S. 29, '51. Is Hollywood through? Samuel Goldwyn.
Collier's. 128:86. N. 17, '51. Regulation or strangulation?
*Collier's. 131:62-5. Ja. 17, '53. Should Congress be televised? Robert Bendiner.
Columbia Law Review. 51:108-18. Ja. '51. Transit broadcasting.
Commentary. 10:434-8. N. '50. Freedom for radio and TV. J. W. Krutch.
Commercial and Financial Chronicle. Sec2. p 10-11+. O. 19, '50. Television industry. R. A. Graver.
Commercial and Financial Chronical. 173:1325+. Mr. 29, '51. Television's potentialities, progress, and problems. M. C. Faught.
Commercial and Financial Chronicle. 174:2151+. D. 6, '51. Television comes of age. R. D. Siragusa.
Conference Board Business Record. 8:72-4. F. '51. Looking at television now. S. S. Hoffman.

Education. 70:217-24. D. '49. Television and people. Frank Stanton.

Education. 71:599-602. Je. '51. Education by revelation. H. A. Clark:

Education. 72:242-51. D. '51. Television and the high school student. P. A. Witty.

    Same abridged. Journal of Home Economics. 44:293. Ap. '52.

Educational Administration and Supervision. 37:193-210. Ap. '51. Interest in TV and success in school. P. A. Witty.

Educational Administration and Supervision. 38:138-47. Mr. '52. Children's interest in comics, radio, motion pictures, and TV. P. A. Witty.

Educational Record. 33:24-9. Ja. '52. Radio as an educational medium. Doris Corwith.

Educational Record. 33:30-4. Ja. '52. Television as an educational medium. Telford Taylor.

Educational Record. 33:256-60. Ap. '52. Educational television; progress report. Blanche Crippen.

Educational Record. 33:397-402. Jl. '52. Obligations of an educational TV station. Franklin Dunham.

Elementary English. 28:385-91. N. '51. Television and reading. D. B. Gessleman.

    Condensed. Education Digest. 17:43-5. Ja. '52.

Elementary School Journal. 52:129-31. N. '51. Television in education. M. K. Eakin.

English Journal. 39:325-7. Je. '50. Out-of-school radio listening habits of high school students. F. C. Gruber.

English Journal. 40:144-9. Mr. '51. Radio, a means, not an end. Lennox Grey.

English Journal. 40:218-20. Ap. '51. Television, here I come. Lieber Anker.

English Journal. 41:131-6. Mr. '52. What can we do about movies, radio, television? W. D. Boutwell.

English Journal. 41:245-50. My. '52. Effect of radio, television and motion pictures on the development of maturity. S. I. Roody.

Etude. 67:339+. Je. '49. What will television do for music?

Factory Management. 110:110-12. My. '52. TV, newest way to get your story into the home. M. J. Murphy.

Federal Register. 17:3905-4100 (pt II) My. 2, '52. Rules governing television broadcast stations, issued by the Federal Communications Commission.

*Food for Thought. 12:9-15. My. '52. Education for adults on the U.S. air waves. D. F. Greenwood.

Fortune. 44:74-9+. Ag. '51. TV's time of trouble.

Fortune. 44:120-3+. S. '51. Can industry use television?

    Same abridged with title Television in overalls. Reader's Digest. 60:73-5. Ja. '52.

Fortune. 46:86+. S. '52. TV after Chicago.

*Fortune. 46:105+. N. '52. Broadcasters' ordeal by politics. E. H. James.

*Freeman. 2:810. Ag. 25, '52. TV coverage of national conventions. W. S. Schlamm.

George Washington University Law Review. 19:312-35. Ja. '51. Governmental regulation of the program content of television broadcasting. H. E. Forrest.

*Harper's Magazine. 200:51-9. My. '50. Battle over television. John Houseman.

Harper's Magazine. 203:90-4. O. '51. Trial by television. A. T. Klots.

Harper's Magazine. 204:97-9. F. '52. Can unsponsored TV pay its way? B. B. Smith.

Harper's Magazine. 205:82-7. Jl. '52. Radio and the Richards case. Edmund Lawrence.

Harper's Magazine. 205:27-33. N. '52. Politics and TV. Bruce Bliven.

Harvard Business Review. p41-9. My. '52. Future of television. M. C. Faught.

Harvard Education Review. 20:255-70. Fall '50. Television and the schools.
          Bibliography.

Harvard Law Review. 64:727-58. Mr. '51. Recent legislative trends in defamation by radio. D. H. Remmers.

Hollywood Quarterly. 3:248-57. Spring '48. Radio's attraction for housewives. Ruth Palter.

Hollywood Quarterly. 4:256-61. Spring '50. Television in relation to other media. D. W. Smythe.

Hollywood Quarterly. 5:153-63. Winter '50. TV as an art form. Rudy Bretz.

House Beautiful. 92:66-7+. F. '50. What's television going to do to your life? John Crosby.

Journal of Educational Sociology. 24:154-66. N. '50. Problem of television among children. Sigmund Fogler.

Library Journal. 76:567-73, 671-6. Ap. 1-15, '51. What is television doing to public libraries? R. R. Voorhies.

Library Journal. 77:305-6. F. 15, '52. TV and reading report no2. W. H. Kaiser.

*Life. 29:147-8+. N. 6, '50. Seven deadly sins of the air. John Crosby.

Magazine of Wall Street. 90:210-12+. My. 17, '52. Movies: a realistic appraisal. G. L. Merton.

*Measure. 1:209-21. Summer '50. What standards for broadcasting? Sir William Haley.

Nation. 174:inside cover. Mr. 1, '52. Lawmakers on television; Oklahoma legislature. Ray Scales.

Nation. 174:601-3. Je. 21, '52. Morals on your TV. Frank Orme.

National Education Association Journal. 41:367-8. S. '52. Education's fabulous inheritance. P. A. Walker.

Nation's Business. 37:40-2+. Je. '49. TV will change you. Harland Manchester.

Nature. 44:146-8. Mr. '51. Conservation takes to the air. E. A. Cohen.

New Republic. 124:17-24. F. 26, '51. Television and education: panel discussion. Saul Carson and others.

New York State Education. 38:397-400. Mr. '51. TV; problem child or children's pet. F. B. Hennock.

 Condensed. Education Digest. 16:8-10. My. '51.

New York State Education. 39:510-13. Ap. '52. Schools at work on TV. H. F. Partridge.

*New York Times. p X 13. O. 19, '52. Low state of TV. Jack Gould.

*New York Times. p 1+. N. 24, '52. Sherwood to pen nine TV plays. Jack Gould.

New York Times. p 1+. D. 1, '52. House of Representatives opens inquiry on campaign spending. Clayton Knowles.

*New York Times. p X 13. Ja. 11, '53. Educational television in New York state. J. L. Holtzmann.

New York Times. p26. Ja. 23, '53. Eisenhower suggestion for TV press conference. Jack Gould.

*New York Times. p 16. F. 25, '53. Text of report on educational TV stations.

New York Times Magazine. p7+. Je. 12, '49. What is television doing to us? Jack Gould.

New York Times Magazine. p9+. Ja. 28, '51. Finding a place for education on TV. Telford Taylor.

New York Times Magazine. p7+. Je. 24, '51. We can get through the Iron Curtain. Brien McMahon.

New York Times Magazine. p 12+. Ja. 13, '52. Case for televising Congress. J. K. Javits.

New York Times Magazine. p 14+. Mr. 2, '52. Biggest question on TV debates. L. M. Cherne.

New York Times Magazine. p 12-13+. Mr. 9, '52. TV at the crossroads. Jack Gould.

New York Times Magazine. p 14+. Je. 22, '52. X of the campaign: TV personality. Jack Gould.

*New York Times Magazine. p 13+. N. 2, '52. How much has TV changed campaigning? Robert Bendiner.

New York Times Magazine. p50. N. 2, '52. Calmer attitude toward television. Dorothy Barclay.

New Yorker. 27:17-18. Je. 21, '51. Getting tested.

New Yorker. 28:56+. Jl. 19, '52. Republican national convention. Philip Hamburger.

New Yorker. 28:38+. Ag. 2, '52. Coverage of Democratic convention. Philip Hamburger.

Newsweek. 40:66-7. S. 15, '52. FM for the millions.

Ohio Schools. 29:152-3+. Ap. '51. What do children want in radio?
M. C. Koch.

Same condensed. Education Digest. 17:43-4. O. '51.

Ohio State University. Bureau of Educational Research News Letter. 17:
1-4. My. '52. TV—new frontier in education. Edgar Dale.

Parents' Magazine. p36+. D. '50. What shall we do about television?
H. A. Lane.

Phi Delta Kappan. 33:118-21. N. '51. TV's impact on teen-agers.
Philip Lewis.

Printers' Ink.   234:33-5+.   Mr. 9, '51.   Siberia for culture?
exiling educational channels.   Gilbert Seldes.

Printers' Ink. 235:36-7. Je. 9, '51. Will TV kill the movies? W. B.
Laub.

*Printers' Ink. 239:29. Ap. 4, '52. What does the end of the TV freeze
mean? V. J. Dallaire.

Printers' Ink. 239:40. Ap. 18, '52. FCC lifts TV freeze. R. Y. Giles.

Printers' Ink. 239:56+. Je. 13, '52. Case for subscription TV. M. C.
Faught.

Proceedings of the Institute of Radio Engineers. 37:116-23. F. '51.
Television broadcasting in the U. S., 1917-50. D. G. Fink.

Public Opinion Quarterly. 14 no3:461-74. '50. National policy on television. D. W. Smythe.

Public Opinion Quarterly. 14 no4:744-52. '50. Congress on the air.
R. M. Goldman.

Public Opinion Quarterly. 15 no3:421-44. '51. Television, its impact on
school children. E. E. Maccoby.

Public Opinion Quarterly. 15 no4:679. '51. Merchandising commodities
and citizenship on TV. G. W. Wiebe.

Publishers' Weekly. 159:1707-9. 1772-3. Ap. 21-28, '51. Effect of tele -
vision on reading.

Quarterly of Film, Radio and Television. 6:109-28. Winter '51. Consumer's stake in radio and television. D. W. Smythe.

Quarterly of Film, Radio and Television. 6:143-53. Winter '51. Children's television habits and preferences. M. V. Seagoe.

Quarterly of Film, Radio and Television. 7:13-24. Fall '52. Give the
television code a chance. R. D. Swezey.

Quarterly Journal of Economics. 66:194-223. My. '52. Program patterns
and preferences. P. O. Steiner.

Radio and Television News. 45:55+. Mr. '51. United Nations radio.
K. R. Boord.

*Reader's Digest. 59:20-4. Jl. '51. Must we all join the captive audi-
ence? Holman Harvey.

Recreation. 45:189. S. '51. Television, friend or foe? Wayne Coy.
Reply. 45:423. Ja. '52. J. A. Wylie.

Sales Management. 66:81. Ap. 15, '51. Where do people get time for
TV viewing?

Sales Management. 67:45-6+. Jl. 15, '51. What has TV done to other media?

Saturday Evening Post. 221:29+. My. 14, '49. Be good, television's watching. R. M. Yoder.

*Saturday Evening Post. 224:30+. Ag. 25, '51. What about pay-as-you-look TV? Victor Ullman.

Saturday Evening Post. 224:17-19+, 30+, 30+. Ja. 19, Ja. 26, F. 2, '52. Big brawl: Hollywood v. television. Milton MacKaye.

Saturday Evening Post. 224:28-9+. Ja. 26, '52. Hole in the Iron Curtain. Richard Thruelson.

Saturday Evening Post. 225:28-9+. Jl. 5, '52. Watch your step at the conventions. Hugh Morrow.

*Saturday Review. 35:30-1. Mr. 15, '52. Politics, televised and sponsored. Gilbert Seldes.
    Reply with rejoinder. 35:24. Ap. 26, '52. P. R. Levin.

*Saturday Review. 35:16+. S. 13, '52. World floods into Iowa. R. L. Shayon.

Saturday Review. 35:35-6. S. 20, '52. Commercial as a work of art. Gilbert Seldes.

*Saturday Review of Literature. 32:20. D. 24, '49. Time-trap. Norman Cousins.

*Saturday Review of Literature. 34:7-8+. Ag. 25, '51. Television with a conscience. William Benton.

Saturday Review of Literature. 34:24+. N. 3, '51. Can TV survive advertising? Raymond Rubicam.

*Saturday Review of Literature. 34:25+. N. 3, '51. It's still a business. M. B. Mitchell.

School and Society. 74:369-72. D. 15, '51. Television and the educative progress. P. A. Witty.
    Bibliography.
    Same condensed. Educational Digest. 17:6-9. Mr. '52.

*School and Society. 74:374-6. D. 15, '51. Instruction by television and home study. J. P. Barden.

School and Society. 75:70-2. F. 2, '52. Literature on television. Joseph Remenyi.

School Arts. 51:158-60+. Ja. '52. Art in educational television. A. W. Randall.

School Life. 34:88-9+. Mr. '52. Effect of television on school achievement of children. Franklin Dunham.
    Bibliography.

School Life. 34:136-7+. Je. '52. FCC television decision.

School Review. 60:322-4. S. '52. Education by television. H. A. Anderson.

Science Digest. 30:77-80. N. '51. Pay as you see television. W. H. Oxstein.

Scientific American. 184:15-17. Je. '51. Analysis of television programs. D. W. Smythe.

*Senior Scholastic. 57:20-1. S. 20, '50. TV: enemy of education? H. L. Marx, Jr.

Senior Scholastic. 58:12-13. My. 2, '51. Prying eye of television.

Senior Scholastic (Teacher ed.) 58:22T. My. 2, '51. Our 121 educational stations. W. J. Temple.

Senior Scholastic. 59:7-9. Ja. 16, '52. Invisible front.

Senior Scholastic. 60:7-9. F. 12, '52. Eyes on Congress; should sessions of Congress be televised?

*Senior Scholastic. 61:5-6. O. 29, '52. Which way for educational TV? Harold Brown.

Social Studies. 41:214+. My. '50. Television faces society. Benjamin Rowe.

Sociology and Social Research. 35:113-22. N. '50. Television and the family. E. C. McDonagh and others.

State Government. 24:209-11. Ag. '51. Educational television. E. J. McGrath.

*State Government. 24:249-50+. O. '51. Televising the legislature in Oklahoma. Paul Harkey.

Survey. 86:4-9. Ja. '50. Television, hopes and limitations. C. A. Siepmann.

Survey. 86:482-6. N. '50. Social impact of television. Frank Riley and J. A. Peterson.

*Survey. 87:259-61. Je. '51. Listeners' radio, why not? Jerry Voorhis.

Survey. 87:455-9. N. '51. "This is the Voice of America." Hillier Krieghbaum.

Tele-Tech. 11:38-9. Ja. '52. Milestones of thirty years of radio-TV development, 1922-51.

Tennessee Planner. 11:110-19. F. '51. Radio's role in defense. Charles Heslep.

*Theatre Arts. 36:26-8+. Ap. '52. Pay as you view TV. Fred Hift.

Theatre Arts. 36:36-7+. My. '52. Radio grows up. Harriet Van Horne.

Town Meeting (Bulletin of America's Town Meeting of the Air). 16, no31:1-16. N. 28, '50. Who should be responsible for education on television? F. B. Hennock and others.

Town Meeting (Bulletin of America's Town Meeting of the Air). 16, no42:1-13. F. 13, '51. Is television an asset or liability to education? C. A. Siepmann and others.

Town Meeting (Bulletin of America's Town Meeting of the Air). 17, no40:1-16. Ja. 29, '52. Should Congress be televised? W. F. Bennett and J. K. Javits.

United States News & World Report. 31:38-44. N. 9, '51. What's next in television? David Sarnoff.

United States News & World Report. 32:65-6+. Ap. 11, '52. TV, biggest boom ahead.

United States Office of Education Bulletin. 1952, no 16:1-34. '52. Television in our schools. Franklin Dunham and R. R. Lowdermilk.

Vital Speeches of the Day. 17:413-6. Ap. 15, '51. Television: phonevision. M. C. Faught.

Western Advertising. p37-8+. N. '50. Television's current and future prospects. R. C. Francis.

39058

Marx, H. L.
                              HE
                             8698

Television and radio in American
   life.
                             .M3
'81   (30 issues)

DATE	ISSUED TO
AUG 2 0 1986	Amy Lehmann
NOV 1 1 1986	Karl Burns
FEB 2 4 1987	Dawn Welkie
PR 2 8 1987	Wendy Falk
MY 1 9 92	DAWN S.
MY 1 0 '94	Bess Pabin

39058   HE
                               8698
                               .M3

SPEECH AND DEBATING

Competitive Debate: Rules and Strategy. By G. M. Musgrave. 151p. rev. ed. 1946. $1.25.

Discussion Methods: Explained and Illustrated. By J. V. Garland. 376p. 3d ed. rev. 1951. $3.

Extempore Speaking: A Handbook for the Student, the Coach, and the Judge. By D. L. Holley. 115p. 1947. $1.50.

High School Forensics: An Integrated Program. By A. E. Melzer. 153p. 1946. 90c.

How to Debate. By H. B. Summers, F. L. Whan, and T. A. Rousse. rev. ed. 349p. 1950. $2.75.

Representative American Speeches. By A. C. Baird, comp. Published annually in The Reference Shelf. Prices vary.

Each volume contains representative speeches by eminent men and women on public occasions during the year. Each speech is prefaced by a short sketch of the speaker and the occasion.

Selected Readings in Rhetoric and Public Speaking. By Lester Thonssen, comp. 324p. 1942. $3.50.